THE
AVENGERS
AND ME

"But Patrick, you're always doing The Avengers!"
Peter O'Toole, 1977

STARRING

STARRING
PATRICK
MACNEE
AS JOHN STEED

DIANA
RIGG

PRODUCED BY
JULIAN
WINTLE

THE AVENGERS

AND ME

PATRICK MACNEE
WITH DAVE ROGERS

TV Books

TV BOOKS • NEW YORK

THE AVENGERS AND ME
ISBN: 1-57500-059-8

TV Books, L.L.C.
Publishers serving the television industry.
1619 Broadway, Ninth Floor
New York, NY 10019
www.tvbooks.com

Distributed to the trade by HarperCollins Publishers.

Designed by Paul Chamberlain.

Publisher's Cataloging-in-Publication Data
Macnee, Patrick, 1922–
        The Avengers and me / Patrick Macnee, Dave Rogers. — 1st ed.
    p. cm.

        1. Macnee, Patrick, 1922– 2. Avengers (Television program) 3. Actors—Great Britain—
Biography. I. Roger, Dave. II. Title.

    PN1992.77.A923M33 1998   791.45'028'092
                                                                  QBI98–10507

First US edition.
Originally published by Titan Books, London, UK.

Dedicated to:
Albert Fennell and Julian Wintle.

THANKS AND ACKNOWLEDGEMENTS:

Many thanks for the contributions from (in alphabetical order)
Ray Austin, Charles Crichton, Desmond Davis, Robert Day, Peter Hammond, Richard Harris, Richard Hatton, Gareth Hunt, Laurie Johnson, Don Leaver, Roger Marshall, Sydney Newman, Harry Pottle, Peter Graham Scott, Don Sharp and Julie Stevens.

I would also like to thank the following people and organisations for their invaluable help: *Variety*, *Stage & Television Today*, *Daily Sketch*, *London Evening News*, *Daily Express*, *The Sun*, British Broadcasting Company (*The Critics* BBC Home Service March 1963, with Harry Craig). For the photographs: John Herron (UGC), Gilly Hartley (Thames TV), Laurie Johnson (Avengers Film & TV Ent Ltd), Brian Clemens, Julie Stevens, Joy and Stephen Curry, Howard Lee, Harry Pottle, Adrian Rigelsford, Gordon Hendry, John Blocher (Cornerstone Communications Ltd), Gary Leigh (*Dreamwatch*) and Marcus Hearn.

CONTENTS

Recently I boarded a ship at Tilbury docks in London and went on a cruise to St. Petersburg, Russia. There were 1,000 passengers on board, and 645 of them, approximately, came up during the voyage and introduced themselves to me, saying how fondly they remembered Steed in *The Avengers* and *The New Avengers*.

Since I'm now old, and fat, and grey, I'm not sure I was altogether flattered! Most of them said they recognized me by my voice!

Seriously, I am deeply grateful that they remember me at all. It's very nice to be paid a compliment like that and to realize that after all these years one is remembered for what was, and still is, a rattling good show.

Now, thirty-seven years later, Warner Brothers has decided to make a big-screen movie of *The Avengers*. I was fortunate enough, on the first day of shooting in June 1997, to meet the star, Ralph Fiennes.

He was wearing a smartly-cut, three-piece suit, sported a bowler hat and carried a rolled-up umbrella!

I was surprised. I had not expected him to wear such stylized clothes in the realistic nineties. I asked him if he was going to carry a gun. "Oh no," he said, "I'm going to play it just like *you* did—although, of course, there is only *one* Steed."

I was deeply touched by the compliment.

As it happens, the original film negatives of "The Avengers"—episodes of which have been seen on TV throughout the world during the last twenty-five years with bits missing all over the place and sub-standard visual and sound clarity—have now been *digitally restored* to their original quality, with *no* edits. Seeing them again has made me a very happy man. They are something to be proud of once more.

Now, with videocassettes set for distribution in the USA and throughout the world soon, 1998 promises to be a vintage year for *The Avengers* on all fronts.

Dave Rogers and I decided to collaborate on this book to recall what it was actually like to spend ten years, on and off, as John Steed—a character I created from the meager description in the script for the first *Avengers* story: "Steed stands there." That's all it said about the character I was supposed to play. Just that! No description! No background detail—nothing!

Three decades later, I'm delighted that *The Avengers* is moving into the nineties.

Patrick Macnee

**Patrick Macnee
January 1998**

PREFACE

I spent eight years, between 1952 and 1960, in Hollywood, New York and Toronto, doing live television, scrabbling for every bit of work I could get. Stage roles, bit parts in radio and television: I tackled them all.

I played in *The Moonstone* with Christopher Plummer, for a tiny radio company called the CBC, which was about to branch out into television. I worked with people like Lorne Greene, Barry Morse and William Shatner, who happened to be around at the same time. We did plays and television together.

I was in the first television play ever produced in Canada. I worked for a man named David Greene, who went on to win five Emmys, one of them for *Roots*. (It's true to say, I think, that David invented the television mini-series.)

I did live television in New York, with people like George Roy Hill. The most famous was a version of *A Night to Remember*, about the sinking of the *Titanic*. That was in 1956, and we performed it live from the studio. Studios didn't have special effects departments then... well, I suppose they did, but they were very primitive. We sunk the *Titanic* in a fish tank!

Then I went to see a clairvoyant at Huntington Beach, California. He told me that my fortunes would improve if I returned to London.

Having made a little bit of money from acting in *The Importance of Being Earnest* with Dame Edith Evans, on television in Toronto, I boarded a plane and landed in London in April 1960 with just $400 to my name.

A couple of months later, I was walking along Piccadilly. It was teeming with rain and I sidled along, stopping every now and then to take shelter in shop doorways. A short distance before I reached Piccadilly Circus, I passed Millets, a store which sold mackintoshes and distinctly English clothes. Out of it stepped a man wearing a brand new raincoat, the belt of which was tied loosely around his waist. I recognised him instantly. His name was Edgar Peterson, a big Hollywood producer. The last time I'd seen him had been in Hollywood, at a funeral at the Westwood Memorial Park.

"Patrick," he exclaimed, "you're just the man I need!"

Intrigued, I asked him what for. He explained that he wanted me to become his producer.

"What of?" I enquired. He replied that he was doing a western.

"What, *here*?" I asked, somewhat confused. A *western*, filmed in England?

He nodded.

"What's it about?"

His reply came as something of a surprise.

"It's about Winston Churchill. I'd like you to produce the British end of the project."

I gulped, and he invited me to the Savoy Hotel for a drink.

At that time I was grateful to anybody who offered to buy me a drink, and Peterson was offering me a job as well! It was a bolt straight from the blue or, seeing as how the heavens had opened in earnest by now, straight from the thunder-threatening clouds.

Above: My years as John Steed were still to come...

Opposite: Circa 1960, just months away from becoming an Avenger.

THE VALIANT YEARS

Earl Mountbatten asked if we knew the famous story of Sir Winston chatting about Far East policy with him while luxuriating in a foam-filled bath, smoking a large Corona cigar.

The mere fact that I, this scruffy, ill-kempt looking person, was being brought into The Savoy, was rather like a sinner being admitted into heaven. Peterson led me into the grill-room, ordered two large scotch and sodas, and we talked about the job.

Some time later, we were joined by Victor Wolfson, who was a very experienced Hollywood screenwriter. We chatted together. Peterson and Wolfson exuded an air of confidence and I was astounded to learn that their partner, Jack Le Vien, had signed a contract with Sir Winston.

The originator of the idea, Jack Le Vien had been to the south of France to see Churchill. He took along a lovely cage with a budgerigar in it, which the old man took to, and eventually persuaded Sir Winston to give him the rights to his own story of the Second World War, taken from his memoirs. Le Vien planned to turn this into a television series called *The Valiant Years*.

So I became a producer... well, I was really the head of the London production staff, a researcher, but I *thought* that I was a producer. I took an office in Jermyn Street, just off Piccadilly Circus, and settled in with two of Sir

Winston's former secretaries and Lord Portal's daughter — Portal had been the head of the Royal Air Force. She was a fine lady and my trusted lieutenant throughout the whole enterprise. We employed a team of writers to get the project together and worked extremely hard from about May 1960.

Newsreel footage of actual events was to be used throughout the series and we had a distinguished man named Anthony Bushell to help me direct the interviews with the military people who had worked with Churchill.

As Bushell was Sir Laurence Olivier's main 'lieutenant' (he'd been associate producer on *Hamlet* and many other things), we originally asked Olivier to speak Sir Winston's words. He asked for £100,000. Too much — so we got Richard Burton for £10,000.

After a short while, Edgar Peterson got terribly megalomaniacal and started to wire ABC Television in New York. Several distinguished people were running ABC at that time, one of whom was Dan Melnick, the son-in-law of Richard Rodgers, who was composing the musical score for *The Valiant Years*. Peterson had wired Melnick the message, 'Too much

John Schlesinger
at work.

music!' The composer's son-in-law wired back, 'Never mind the music... You're fired!'

So Peterson tottered off the scene, shattered and shaken, and went back to the United States, leaving me, an inexperienced novice at the production game, basically in charge of the whole caboodle. Then Tony Bushell left to do some work for Olivier and I had the task of replacing him. I immediately thought of John Schlesinger, who was my next door neighbour in Berkshire.

I asked John if he was interested. He explained that he'd already been approached and wanted to do it, so we started to knock the thing into shape. We got the screenplay together and in a very short space of time were shooting interviews with Admirals, Air Commodores, Field Marshals Alanbrook, Montgomery, Slim and Earl Mountbatten.

Never having conducted any interviews before, the thought of being in the presence of these great men — men who had actually *made* history — was terrifying. Having been just a naval lieutenant in the war, it was extraordinary to be working with such talented, legendary people. It was a great honour to do so.

All were filmed in settings that existed during the war. Lord Slim gave his account in the actual War Room under the Ministry of Defence building. Taken aback when I asked him to describe the Burma campaign in three minutes, I recall that he looked at the map I'd placed on a wall and said, "You've got the Irrawaddy river in the wrong place, Macnee!"

Earl Mountbatten I found immensely cooperative. John Schlesinger and I turned up at the Ministry of Defence to be met by a very smart ADC, who escorted us to his Lordship's office. Mountbatten had decided to do the interview in another office, and was being made-up by a young female naval rating. He talked most of the time and asked us if we knew the famous story of Sir Winston chatting about Far East policy with him while luxuriating in a foam-filled bath, smoking a large Corona cigar. We confessed that we didn't.

John Schlesinger filmed an unforgettable interview with an able seaman, one of the three survivors from the battleship HMS *Hood*. I had tears in my eyes when he told us his story of what happens as a ship goes down fighting. John developed his unique talent of

John Schlesinger at work.

Sydney Newman.

realistic cinema on these interviews. These were given facing directly to camera, which at that time was a first. John just sat beside the camera and asked the interviewees to talk. He was a master at extracting recall, memory, affection and warmth from all these dear people who had served throughout this devastating war — as had John and myself, both of us in the Navy.

I remember that we didn't pay these remarkably talented people much for their time — seventy-five quid or something, not much more — but Lord Alanbrook was delighted with the fee as it allowed him to renovate his cottage roof. John Schlesinger told me later that Viscount Montgomery had only agreed to do the interview if we paid him £500, which was to be donated to the indigent families of the clergy.

I was told to forget about interviewing Odette Churchill. "She won't talk! Too many people have accused her of not doing the things she says she has done."

I decided that the only way to approach her was to get her into conversation with someone who had been subjected to similar experiences. I selected René Burdet, a Frenchman, the John Steed *par excellence* of the French Resistance.

Owner of a small London hotel at the time, he was delighted to help. Accepting René's dinner invitation, over steaks and claret, and prompted by René's, "Do you remember when...?" recollections, Odette Churchill gave us an amazing interview.

———

A few months went by and I was feeling rather pleased with myself. I was now a businessman... I was becoming a *producer*! Full of myself, I believed that I was really very efficient.

The fact that I was nowhere near as efficient as I thought was suddenly brought home when John Schlesinger started sending frantic cables to Dan Melnick in New York saying, 'You'll have to fire Macnee, he doesn't really seem to know what he's doing!'

When I heard about this (fortunately within hours of what I viewed as an act of perfidy by a man whom I had employed), I dictated a letter of defence to my secretary which she wired to New York — the upshot being that Dan Melnick flew in from the States.

Gathered together in my office, Melnick spoke first.

"I've received your cable, John. I've read your defence, Pat," he said. "Which of these am I going to listen to? Which do I take action on?"

John responded first: "Well, what Macnee wants me to do is so bloody trivial. He keeps sending me off to photograph these ridiculous things, like Sir Winston's shoes in Bond Street. I'm a *director* and I want to do important things. We're interviewing these extremely important people. He comes along and stands there in awe! It's bloody madness!"

John's opinion might well have been right — I was certainly flying by the seat of my pants — but I *thought* I knew what I was doing. Listening to this, I was absolutely quivering inside, terrified that this prestigious project was slipping away. I took a deep breath, drew myself up to my full height, and said:

"Mr Melnick, I'm doing what you told me to do. I've kept this production in order, despite Mr Peterson leaving. I've been here from the start. *I*, in fact, was largely instrumental in getting Mr Schlesinger this job and I do not take kindly to being cut up in front of my employer, particularly when I think I'm doing a good job. Please, Mr Melnick, view this thing from both sides."

John stood there puffing and tutting, but I won. I stuck with the job until I wanted to leave — and did leave for *The Avengers*. Our differences aside, I had a great affection for John, and, of course, ever since enormous admiration. I was privileged to work with him. A short time later, John directed the documentary *Terminus*, about twenty-four hours in the life of Waterloo Station, a brilliant piece of work awarded the Golden Lion at the Venice Film Festival.

———

Some weeks later I went out to dinner with Leonard White...

It happened like this. Two Toronto friends, Toby Robins and Bill Freedman, called me up and asked if I would like to visit the theatre.

"What are you seeing?" I asked. They'd booked tickets for *A Passage to India* at the Comedy Theatre. I'd already seen *Passage* and suggested *A Man for All Seasons*. They were seeing that the following night, so we agreed to meet during the interval at the Comedy, just off the Haymarket in London's West End.

With them at the theatre was Leonard White, another friend from my time in Canada. I'd looked on him as a good, burgeoning actor. He'd been in *The White Devil* and *The Sleep of Prisoners* with me — a lot of shows, including another wonderful Christopher Fry play, *The Lady's Not for Burning*. I'd known him for years. We had spent many happy times together visiting the YMCA for workouts when I was living in a garret on Prince Arthur Avenue in Toronto.

So when they came out during the interval and Bill said that the play was terribly boring, I asked him to join me for the last act of *A Man for All Seasons*. He was happy to do so, but Toby and Leonard preferred to stay. I suggested the four of us meet up later at an Italian restaurant near the Coliseum in St Martin's Lane. Bill and I raced off and were able to get standing room only tickets for the last act of *A Man for All Seasons*, a marvellous play which had the Common Man played by Leo McKern and Paul Scofield as Sir Thomas More, a truly great role for which he later won an Oscar.

We met as arranged and during the course of the evening, I turned to Leonard White and asked what he was doing. He explained that he was working for a man called, "... Well, what am I saying, Patrick? You know him — Syd Newman."

I remembered Sydney Newman. He had been one of the pioneer heads of CBC drama and was the boss of everything in Toronto. You couldn't turn left or right in Canada without bumping into him in the television studios. Leonard explained that he was now a revolutionary force for ABC Television in England and was doing a series called *Armchair Theatre*, a prestigious, highbrow collection of plays which had set a new standard for television drama. But that wasn't all...

"He's got this series called *Police Surgeon*, with an actor called Ian Hendry. They're changing it and calling it *The Avengers*," Leonard said. "They're going to get somebody else in with him and make it more of a genuine action adventure series. Would you be interested in doing it? They're going to try it out over Christmas."

"When does it start?" I asked.

He said that they were due to start in November. "They'll run it for three months. If it's popular it will go on. If it isn't, it won't."

I told Leonard that I wasn't too sure about acting in a television series. I was doing an awfully good job at that moment — a solid job. He asked how much it paid.

I told him fifty quid a week. He grinned and said that I'd get a little more than that if I was starring in a television series.

"Oooh, I see," I said. My interest aroused, I asked him to have Sydney Newman call me.

So, the next morning I went back to my office

in Jermyn Street and over coffee asked Tony Bushell how much he thought I should ask for.

His reply shook me. I shouldn't do it for a penny less than £300.

"My God," I thought, thinking that Tony was quite mad — £300! I couldn't possibly ask for that. However, when Sydney Newman telephoned me to see if I wanted to be involved, that's exactly what I asked for.

"£300!" he gasped.

There was a moment of silence. Then, to my utter astonishment, he said okay. Of course, what he meant was £300 an episode. I meant £300 a *week*. I didn't get it. I got £150 a week. I didn't have an agent at the time, so I signed for £300 every two weeks — far better than the £50 a week I was being paid on the Churchill series, which was nearing completion anyway.

So I got myself out of *The Valiant Years*, on which I was really an extremely ordinary producer and couldn't make the books balance. I never could do anything like that. I think they breathed a sigh of relief and were glad to see the back of me.

Thus the direction of my future was settled. At the time, of course, I had absolutely no idea as to how or why *The Avengers* came to be.

Sydney Newman provides the answer:

'The story of the creation of *The Avengers* is typical of most creative efforts, in that it is in essence a group activity in which every part interacts, and the whole interacts with its social environment. Nothing proves this more than the idea which I originated, made real by dozens of talents and unavoidable influences outside the group. As you will see, it started out as something not so very different from the Steed/Emma Peel series, which is still popular worldwide.

'In 1959, I think it was, as Head of Drama for ABC Television, which had the Saturday and Sunday franchise for London, the Midlands and the North, I was visited by Felix de Wolfe, an agent, and a writer I didn't know personally. He was Julian Bond, whose stuff on another commercial station I admired for its earnest feel. Felix, in a masterful pitch, sold me on a good idea for a potentially popular half-hour series devised by his client. It was a great idea, he said, because it "amalgamates the ideas of two of the most popular dramas running on the air — *Dixon of Dock Green* and *Emergency Ward Ten*, cops and doctors." What could be better, said the crass, commercial side of me. It was easy to see that the hero, a doctor, while administering to someone who'd been shot, could easily get involved, find evidence the police had missed, follow it up and solve the crime. His dramatic bailiwick could range from the slums to Mayfair.

'The tricky part of the deal was that Julian Bond, a writer, also wished to be the show's producer. That worried me, but I figured that by training him myself and giving him experienced support, the idea was worth a gamble. My boss, Managing Director Howard Thomas, agreed and secured a thirteen week run on the network. Thus a half-hour series called *Police Surgeon* was born about a doctor who, as part of his practice, is on first call by the police. Julian, with the help of Dodo Watts, our brilliant casting director, found Ian Hendry, a relatively unknown actor for the lead role of Dr Geoffrey Brent, the police surgeon of the title.

'After four shows Julian left, saying he'd rather write than produce. The grubby budgetary disciplines and emotional tantrums of the variety of talents were not for him — something I quite well understood. What a mess.

'I needed a producer in a hurry and recalled an Englishman, Leonard White, an amiable chap and also a first-class stage director who had become a television director at the CBC in Canada. Now back in England, he dropped into my office to say hello. I decided, again, to gamble on an untrained TV producer and phoned him to ask if he would take on the job for the final nine shows. "No," he said, "I want to direct. But since I'm free and if you think I can do it, yes, I'll take it on." That appointment turned out to be one of the best I ever made.

'A chunky looking man with prominent jaw-bones that suggested stubbornness, Leonard turned out to be a good leader, open-minded while retaining his own, and able to convince others of his sound opinions: the mark of a good producer. In addition, he knew more about theatre, acting and direction than I did by far.

'While *Police Surgeon* was pretty good, it somehow didn't take off. My own opinion was that it was on the air at the wrong time — 7.00pm, Saturday night. But one thing was very clear to both me and Leonard — Ian Hendry was a potential star and I was in a hurry to capitalise on his popularity. I felt that people liked his everyday good looks that radiated integrity, observable intelligence and a kind of innocence.

'So, I determined to exploit Hendry's qualities in a one-hour series, as a character who was honourable and had great physical dexterity. It would be a fun series that would get away from the realism of *Police Surgeon* (something which my major series *Armchair Theatre* was noted for). This had to be different: melodramatic, an action adventure-thriller with a sense of humour. I felt that I could capitalise on the current, literary popularity of the John Le Carré/Ian Fleming genre and send it up. Why not make fun of the whole 'spy' non-

sense? I was getting somewhere.

'However, a series based on one character, shot live every week, would be too great a burden on him. I needed a second character. To contrast Hendry's integrity and his physical presence, I thought of teaming him with an undercover agent, an MI5 type, someone he *wouldn't* approve of. Someone amoral, suave and brainy, who wouldn't deign to dirty himself by physically fighting, preferring a silenced gun or sword-cane. Sparks would fly between them. Leonard White liked the idea and agreed to remain as its producer. But who would play the suave spy?

'Fortunately, back in England was Patrick Macnee, whom I knew moderately well in Canada when I was running TV drama for the Canadian Broadcasting Corporation. He had been in dozens of my productions playing all sorts of characters that didn't deny his good looks. A guy who potentially was exactly what I wanted — and I *got* him.' ∎

Sydney Newman: "Ian Hendry was a potential star, and I was in a hurry to capitalise on his popularity."

I was asked to visit Teddington Studios a few weeks later. There to meet me were Sydney Newman and Leonard White, whom I knew, and Ian Hendry and Don Leaver, whom I didn't. Don Leaver, who would be directing the first show, handed me a script. I scanned through it — it wasn't very good.

The press had been invited and we did a publicity shoot, with Ian and myself photographed wearing raincoats and smoking cigarettes. I had been on the *Dane Clark Show* in Hollywood in the fifties and couldn't help wondering why all heroes in TV action series have to wear raincoats, slouch hats and smoke cigarettes?

We started to rehearse the series in a second storey room above The Tower, in Hammersmith. It was Monday 28 November 1960, four weeks before the first episode (a two-parter) was to be recorded on 30 December. This was to be my home, on and off, for the best part of a year.

On the very first day, we sat down with Don Leaver and heard the opening bars of a theme written for the show by a famous jazz musician called Johnny Dankworth. If Don's intention was to get us into the mood of the piece and ease the first day's tension, it failed to achieve the desired effect.

A few minutes into the reading, Ian Hendry plonked his bottom on a chair and said, "It's crap. This is all *crap!*"

Don looked at him. Whatever did he mean? Ian said, "It doesn't work, does it? It just doesn't work!" He suddenly tore the whole of the script in half (a terribly difficult thing to do). "It's crap," he snarled. "It's a load of crap!"

I just sat there wondering what the hell was going on.

Sydney Newman wasn't there. He was in the studio doing an *Armchair Theatre* presentation with one of his distinguished group of directors, people like Ted Kotcheff, Philip Saville and David Greene. *The Avengers*, I guess, was looked on as just another series.

But Ian Hendry did not view it that way. He viewed it in terms of character relationships. Everything had depth as far as Ian was concerned. Dogmatic, he treated the writers as hacks, which was a brilliant idea because it stirred them up, made them furious and so everybody came in with their creative juices really flowing.

Don Leaver remembers that time:

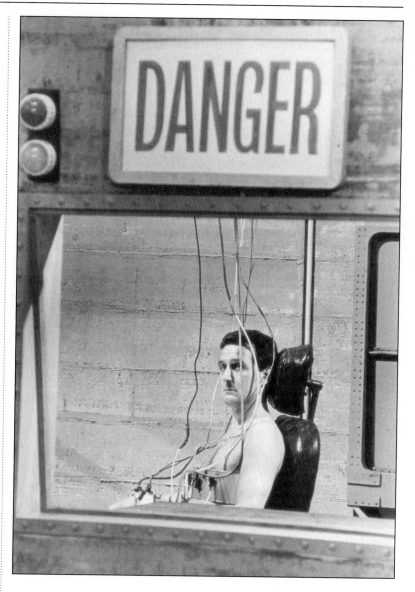

Above: Threatened with a shock exit in 'Dragonsfield'.

Opposite: With Ian, dressed in the compulsory raincoat, smoking the obligatory cigarette.

'Ian's outbursts did result in a lot of rewriting on the rehearsal floor, not always, I fear, for the best — but often so. All of us found Ian to be a very exciting actor and we were not surprised when Sydney announced that we were going on to make a wonderful new show by teaming Ian up with Patrick Macnee. "Patrick *who*?" we asked. Both Sydney and Leonard had known Patrick in Canada, but to the rest of the team appointed to work on the new show he was a totally unknown quantity, so we awaited the arrival of this mystery man with bated breath. Imagine the general surprise when Patrick at his most urbane and British turned up — it's

TWO MEN IN RAINCOATS

'The Springers'.

fair to say that we were gobsmacked. We felt that a quick trawl through *Spotlight* could have produced a similar actor. We were, however, quite wrong and should have trusted Sydney's formidable instinct, because it was very soon apparent that there was a great chemistry between Ian and Pat. They were very complementary together, each supplying aspects that the other might have been lacking.'

Ian's comments were passed back to the producer. The script was rewritten, incorporating many of the ideas he'd suggested. Concerned that viewers tuning into the new series might confuse Doctor Dent (Ian's character as it was defined in the first draft) with the Doctor Brent he had played in *Police Surgeon*, Ian suggested that the character be given a new name. The character became Doctor Keel. Steed, of course, was always Steed.

Sydney Newman relates how, together with Leonard White, he overcame the dilemma of introducing the new concept to the viewers — vital, of course, if the audience was to accept

the justification behind the teaming of Keel and Steed as *The Avengers*:

'To solve the problem of bringing together these two disparate characters — Hendry, the moral innocent, and Macnee, the amoral sophisticate — we set it up that Hendry's fiancée is accidentally shot by a killer aiming at Hendry. Just as a second try is attempted, the killer is foiled by a mysterious stranger who emerges from the shadows — Patrick's John Steed, who offers to assist Hendry in finding the killer.

'I never liked the title of the series. The idea of revenge offended my Canadian sensibility — morally wrong. But after Leonard, myself, Patrick Brawn (the designated story editor) and young John Bryce spent weeks of sweating out dozens of titles, trying them out on anyone in sight, I reluctantly settled on *The Avengers*.

'Howard Thomas supported me, as he usually did, but had trouble selling it to the entire commercial network. ATC, London's station run by the charming but obdurate Lew Grade, refused to take it, but the other stations did and, produced live, it miraculously went on the air a record five weeks after *Police Surgeon* ended. *The Avengers* built audiences so rapidly that ten weeks after it began, Lew Grade changed his mind and so Londoners began to see and enjoy it as the rest of Britain did. Audiences didn't just watch it in massive numbers, they positively loved it.

'The Avengers' popularity rested on more than the surface excitement of the fast pace. The series had that most precious, enticing element: the humour which came from Hendry's near priggish suspicion of Macnee's sophistication and lack of morals as he gets sucked into one adventure after another, each actor contributing inventive bits of business to enlarge the scriptwriters' work.

'The show gained enormously from the original eye of director Peter Hammond, with his unusual camera angles, depth of field and crotch-level shots, and Don Leaver's inventive characterisations.'

So that first episode was played as though it was something by Graham Greene or... well, I really don't know quite who, but that's what made the show, in that everybody in it was not quite what they appeared to be — even though we were actually doing a completely straightforward piece.

The critics, however, were not impressed:

'As an opener, it failed to establish convincing motivation for the central characters and the careful realism of its settings and dialogue threw into relief the trumped-up machinations of the plotting,' claimed an Associated Press review published in *Variety*. 'Keel just seemed a dope for falling for Steed's advice without asking a few obvious questions. And Steed's ambiguity as an undercover man with the gang, yet somehow on the side of the law, just didn't make sense.' *Stage and Television Today* bemoaned the lack of thrills and thought the plot reminiscent of a poor second feature gangster movie. 'There were no thrills, and the clichés thrown up in the ambling wake of the story should make the presenting company blush. Ian Hendry, stern and resolute, was aided by Patrick Macnee, whose style suggests he might be better doing something on his own.'

Ian was an extremely good actor and very, very dedicated. He was equally well dedicated to women and Scotch whisky — traits I shared.

I was very fat at the time. I'd just come off my desk job and had fat cheeks, rather haggard eyes and walked around with a sort of alcoholic blur in front of me because we drank an awful lot. We smoked like chimneys and at the end of each day we'd down several glasses of whisky, ostensibly as a beer chaser.

Ian lived on a boat at the time, *The Two Seas*, which he moored at the Cubitts Yacht Basin,

near Chiswick. It was about three and a half miles away from my characterless little apartment in Stafford Court, just off the Kensington High Street, a short drive from Hammersmith where we did the rehearsals. With the spirit of the night before coursing through our veins, I really can't imagine how we climbed out of bed each morning and arrived at The Tower, fit, glowing and ready to work on the script. Or for that matter, how we got into our cars and tottered back to our homes after a serious night of drinking, particularly from the studios at Teddington, which were some five or six miles from where we lived. But we did. We were always there for rehearsals, and for those truly monstrous two days in front of the camera... of which more later.

Scriptwriter **Richard Harris** was commissioned by Leonard White to write the second script for the show:

'Ian was in the second thing I ever wrote — a play for ABC Television. We became friendly during rehearsals (in those days, you actually had rehearsals) and had the odd pint together.

Steed and Claire (Miranda Connell) are trussed up and gagged in 'The Tunnel of Fear'.

Hot Snow

It has never ceased to amaze me how the writers — Brian Clemens more often than not — manufactured an entertaining way to say goodbye to one of Steed's partners and hello to another.

Spread throughout the book you will find those magical introductions and departures as defined in the scripts.

'Hot Snow' (Episode #1, by Ray Rigby, based on a story by Patrick Brawn).

His fiancée murdered by a gang of heroin smugglers, Dr David Keel vows to track the gang down and avenge her death. His investigations lead him to the flat of a disreputable practitioner.

75 INT. STUDIO. TREADING'S FLAT. FRONT DOOR.
KEEL LOOKS AT DOOR. READS CARD: 'DOCTOR TREADING'. HE IS ABOUT TO PUSH THE BELL BUTTON WHEN THE DOOR IS FLUNG OPEN. STEED STANDS THERE.
KEEL AUTOMATICALLY STEPS BACK A PACE.
KEEL: Doctor Treading?
STEED: Yes. Would you like to come in? You'll find him in there.
HE NODS BACK TO THE INTERIOR, WALKS PAST KEEL AND OUT OF CAMERA. KEEL WATCHES HIM, THEN ENTERS.

76 INT. STUDIO. LIVING ROOM.
A LUXURY FLAT. KEEL ENTERS, LOOKS ABOUT, WAITS. SILENCE. HE MOVES TO DOOR, RINGS BELL, THEN MOVES TO THE MIDDLE OF THE ROOM. WAITS. PUZZLED, HE MOVES TO THE BEDROOM DOOR. KNOCKS, WAITS, THEN OPENS THE DOOR, ENTERS. STOPS IN HIS TRACKS.

77 INT. STUDIO. BEDROOM.
CAMERA ON BODY OF WELL-DRESSED MAN. TWO ATTACHÉ CASES ARE PACKED. ONE ON THE BED, ONE STANDING UPRIGHT ON THE FLOOR. KEEL MOVES INTO ROOM, BENDS DOWN BY BODY. SEES AT A GLANCE THAT THE MAN IS DEAD. EXITS FROM ROOM, CLOSES THE DOOR.

――――――――

122 INT. STUDIO. KEEL'S FLAT. HALL.
KEEL ENTERS. SWITCHES ON LIGHT, CLOSES FRONT DOOR. HANGS UP HAT AND COAT, CROSSES TO LIVING ROOM DOOR.

123 INT. STUDIO. KEEL'S FLAT. LIVING ROOM.
KEEL OPENS DOOR, SWITCHES ON LIGHT, ENTERS. MOVES TO SIDE-BOARD, POURS DRINK. THEN NOTICES THAT ONE OF THE ARM-CHAIRS HAS BEEN MOVED AND NOW FACES THE WINDOW. HE STARES AT IT. CAMERA ON CHAIR AS STEED SLOWLY GETS OUT OF CHAIR, TURNS, FACES CAMERA AND SMILES.
STEED: Good evening.
KEEL: What in blazes are you doing here?
STEED: Waiting to see you. You're back earlier than I expected. How did you get on with the police?
KEEL: How did you get in?
STEED: Through the window. My apologies.
KEEL: Please don't mention it.
STEED: I was very sorry to hear about your fiancée. You know, I think I could be of some assistance to you.

124 INT. STUDIO. KEEL'S FLAT. LIVING ROOM.
KEEL MOVES TO PICK UP PHONE.
KEEL: I think you could be of some assistance to the *police*.
STEED: I shouldn't do that until you've heard what I have to say. Presuming to put myself in your position, if I thought that somebody might be able to help me, I shouldn't throw him out, or have him arrested, until he'd told me what I wanted to know... and if he could lead me to the killer...
KEEL, STONY EYED. STARES AT STEED. TAKES SEAT.
KEEL: Who *are* you?
STEED: I'm very sorry, I can't tell you that — but I'm on the side of the angels, believe me.

KEEL: How do I know?
STEED: You don't, but the police aren't much help are they? As for me — you know I must know *something* or I wouldn't be here... and I imagine you'd rather risk anything than go through the uncertainty of the last three days.
KEEL RISES. MOVES TO SIDEBOARD, POURS DRINKS. HANDS ONE TO STEED. SITS DOWN. STEED SITS OPPOSITE HIM.
KEEL: I might.
STEED: You'd risk your practice? Your reputation?
KEEL: That's impossible to answer.
STEED: Yes, of course it is until you know what it entails.
KEEL: Well, exactly what does it entail?
STEED: You'd have to pretend that it's been your lifelong ambition to push drugs. You're sick of your humdrum practice. You want to make money — lots of money, then retire and live it up on the Continent.
KEEL: And for whose particular benefit is the pretence?
STEED: Various colleagues of mine.
KEEL: These particular colleagues of yours; they're going to trust me?
STEED: Of course not! They don't trust anyone. But I can persuade them to take a chance on you. They'll jump at the opportunity of having a perfectly respectable doctor on the payroll.
KEEL: Oh, I see.
STEED: They are the very best — *doctors*. A consulting room is the perfect warehouse. And then, once you've peddled your first consignment...
KEEL PRETENDS TO IGNORE THIS REMARK.
KEEL: And what is the next move?
STEED: See that you're alone in your surgery at, let's say, 4.30 tomorrow. Would that suit you? You'll have a caller. Not a particularly pleasant person. He will hand you a package and then you are in business.
KEEL: I hesitate to ask, but what am I supposed to do with it?
STEED: Pass it on when you're told to. You may be told quite quickly.

KEEL: And once I've done that I'm in it right up to my ears...
STEED SMILES.
STEED: Exactly!
KEEL: And I will have to do anything they tell me?
STEED: Before you really have to wrestle with your conscience, we'll meet up with the man we both want.
KEEL: *Both*?
STEED: You can take it from me that *I* want that man as much as you.

125 INT. STUDIO. KEEL'S FLAT. LIVING ROOM.
STEED GETS TO HIS FEET. PREPARES TO LEAVE.
STEED: Right, that will have to satisfy you for the moment.
KEEL (SNAPS): I'm afraid that it doesn't!
STEED: It will *have* to, for the time being, Doctor Keel. I'm very sorry but you'll just have to trust me — or not.
KEEL: Thanks for the choice.
STEED: Doctor Keel, do *you* know who killed your fiancée?
KEEL: No, I don't!
STEED: *I do.* And if you don't trust me there isn't a cat in hell's chance of you finding out!

126 INT. STUDIO. KEEL'S FLAT.
LIVING ROOM/HALL (TWO-SHOT)
STEED MOVES TO DOOR. MAKES TO ENTER HALL.
KEEL: Just a minute! How will I keep in contact with you?
STEED: You won't be able to lose me. No, I can see myself out. Goodnight.
STEED EXITS. FRONT DOOR SLAMS. KEEL ENTERS LIVING ROOM, PICKS UP PHONE.

F/U SLIDE F/U GRAMS
"THE AVENGERS" — End of Part 2.
Theme Music.

So began *The Avengers*. ∎

Sent to kill Steed, Spicer (Godfrey Quigley) is taken into custody by The Avengers. A scene from 'Brought to Book', part two of the first story.

In Ian's case, half a pint. When I first met him he drank very little.

'ABC had sense enough to see him for what he was, probably one of the best screen actors we've produced, and gave him a series called *Police Surgeon*. Because Ian had liked my play, he asked if I could contribute to that series, which I did.

'I was living on a barge at the time in a yacht basin in Chiswick. When I first took up residence there, my barge was moored next to a broken-down old boat belonging to an up-and-coming young writer called John Osborne. Ian and his first wife Joanna visited me, liked the idea of living on a boat and bought one. I moved into Ian's old flat in Notting Hill.'

When we weren't drinking, Ian had a twinkle in his eyes for the ladies. He was always turning up with a new girl on his arm, each of whom I found entrancing. I used to get the girls who were really the ones who couldn't get to first base with Ian, of course. Throughout the whole time that we were rehearsing at The Tower, however, I had this darling blonde girl-

friend. We had a chaste but heated love affair and each night I would drive her home to Surbiton. She finally went off to appear in pantomime in Bath and married a dear chap who would make her happy and give her children.

A dark, interesting and very profound man, Ian's technique was wonderful to watch. His insight into character and movement was stimulating, and this shaped the personalities of Keel and Steed, which soon became quite quirky and strange.

We developed the idea of looking at life through the other end of the kaleidoscope, to take things and tilt them on their head. ("The arse-about-face show," I used to call it.) We thought of ways of doing things differently, of attacking the norm. We wanted to excite people, to do something that nobody else had done, to be outrageous.

Early in the series — it may well have been during that first day's rehearsal, I can't remember — Don Leaver asked me if I'd ever read the Bond books by Ian Fleming. I said no. He gave me a copy of the first one, *Casino Royale* (I learned later that the Bond books had been Syd Newman's inspiration when creating some aspects of my character). In this book were scenes of the most unbelievable sadism, horror and beastliness, and graphic descriptions of the villain hitting Bond's testicles with a carpet beater — terrible, ghastly stuff. To my thinking, this seemed to be the opposite of what I was interested in. Bond used women like battering rams and seemed intent on drinking and smoking himself to death. The character I envisaged... well, I hadn't actually thought about Steed in any great detail and was quite undecided as to what to do with him until, after about two or three episodes, Sydney Newman called me into his office and forced me to take stock of my position.

"Patrick," he said, "I'm afraid you're just not working out. You don't seem to *be* anything."

I asked him what I was supposed to be.

"Well, something *interesting*. The part's got no personality. And your clothes... you've got to be more way out. Can't you just go away and think of something?"

I was terribly downtrodden to hear this — I thought that I was doing rather well — and got very angry and stormed out of his office. Depressed, I went home to my flat and thought of how I could improve the character, rationalise it, make it work. I went back to my roots and my father came to mind.

A racehorse trainer, he was a real dandy. He used to lean over the paddock gate, always with a beautiful carnation in his buttonhole. He'd wear a cravat with a pure pearl in it, and wore a lovely brocade waistcoat. The collars of his overcoats were always tailored from ladies'

velvet. Then I 'pinched' a bit from Sir Percy Blakeney, the Scarlet Pimpernel, one of the great British heroes. It seemed to me that if Steed was this shadowy person who was helping to rescue other people, he was something like the Pimpernel — somebody extremely well-dressed who gave the impression of being a fop, so nobody felt that he was a threat. I thought of Bussy Carr, my commanding officer in the Navy. An incredibly brave man, he came from the Carr biscuit family. An amalgam of these three people became Steed. Michael Powell had often called me an eighteenth century man, so I thought of the Regency days — the most flamboyant, sartorially, for men — and I went for that beauteous line in clothing. The ludicrous transformation worked. Sydney Newman went for it and I kept my job! John Steed now had colour and personality.

During the first season, my suits and sports jackets were hired for two guineas and one pound ten shillings respectively. A glance at the wardrobe budget allotment sheet for production 3365 ('Hot Snow') confirms that my raincoat was purchased for twenty-one pounds ten shillings (Ian's trench coat costing eight guineas). Ties, cuff-links, gloves, etc were acquired from the wardrobe people at Teddington. The bowler would arrive a few weeks later. Purchase price, inclusive of remoulding, six pounds two shillings!

A hugely intelligent man, Ian was quite definitely the lead. I was the sort of... second fiddle, if you like. Quite apart from anything else, he was very instructive and very bright, so I *had* to keep on my toes. I just ran along with him in my mackintosh, with a cigarette dangling from my lips, and listened and reacted to his lead — particularly when we had reached our fourth or fifth whisky.

I remember one such occasion mid way through the series, when we were drinking in The Anglers, the pub next door to the studio. He emptied his glass in one gulp and said, "Pat, let's kick the shit out of this thing and make it work!"

"But it does work," I said.

"I don't mean just saying the lines and doing the scenes and the fights," Ian insisted. "Let's get under their skins, see what these

Above: 'Diamond Cut Diamond'.

Opposite above: The rehearsal periods were a grind, and everything was constantly on the move.

Opposite below: Steed arrives in time to rescue his friend from being used as the guinea pig in a deadly experiment. (From 'Dead of Winter'.)

characters *are*."

If nobody else saw the results of this, *we* did. Ian was like that. He was always looking for the *raison d'être* for being there, a theme. And the theme was: let's find things out. Let's be curious.

Curiosity is one of the best dramatic functions there is. To know *how* they did it. *Why* they did it. That's what we had in *The Avengers*. You never quite knew what was going to happen next. You could play with people's emotions, make them wonder what the hell was going on, tickle their curiosity, their sense of suspense. That's what telling the story is, it's narrative, and we had that going for us from the very beginning of the series. We had that... and we did it *live*.

———

I'll describe what live television was like. Firstly you rehearsed in a room, smoking one cigarette after another, and worked out the various scenes... well, the main thing you worked out was how to change your clothes between scenes. When this happened, they used to come in close (with the camera) and focus on a cigarette case or a lamp, anything to give you time to rush to the next set.

After ten days of vivid rehearsal, smoking ourselves silly, drinking at night, learning the lines and rewriting the script, we went into the studio at Teddington and gave a live performance. The Johnny Dankworth theme started us off and into it we went. Then ten days later we did the same thing again.

When you do live television, or a live perfor-

mance which is videotaped for broadcast by the network, the producer sitting in the control box becomes God. He rehearses you for ten days, and then takes you into the studio for you to put it *on camera* — which is a very demeaning thing. You've not really quite learnt it during the ten days in the rehearsal room, because the script and dialogue are constantly changing. So by the time you get to the camera run-through and they tell you not to *act* it, not to *say* it, but to just *move*, so they know where the cameras are going to catch you, you feel totally spare and useless. You ask yourself if you will ever be able to get up to scratch for the show. Nevertheless, you do and, except for two commercial breaks, it goes straight through.

The rehearsal periods were a grind, and I honestly don't know where we managed to get the energy, impetus or the skill and panache when it came to acting on camera. Even though it took ages to set the cameras up so that they arrived at the right spot or went through the right door or shot us in the right light, when it was being filmed live we could not stop, even if the camera was missing or was reflected in a mirror or something, which occasionally it was.

Everything was constantly on the move, except for the producer and the script editor, who just focused on what was happening on the screen, or the director, who sat in the sound booth, having already set out the angles and placement of the cameras during the run-through.

Peter Hammond in particular was a genius at this. He had an iron control over his camera team, five or six of whom had been at Teddington for a long time and were hugely talented. Peter always got the best out of them, although they were immensely creative people in their own right. The camera team had nerves of steel. They were always on the move and were unerringly accurate when it came to getting the huge, heavy cameras to the designated spot on the studio floor.

We didn't know how well we'd done or how it had gone. We had no feeling. We just raced into it, through it and out of it, but I was immensely used to this by now. I'd been working solidly since 1956 in live television. I'd acted on *Playhouse 90* in Hollywood, the *Kraft Hour*, and the *Johnson Hour* in New York. Lots of programmes, with all sorts of actors and directors, so I was used to this catch-as-catch-can type of live television. I'd had so much experience that I was able to inject some sort of personality into it.

I don't know what it was. Peter Hammond didn't know what it was, even though he'd been an actor himself — a very good comedy actor. He'd appeared in *Holiday Camp*, with

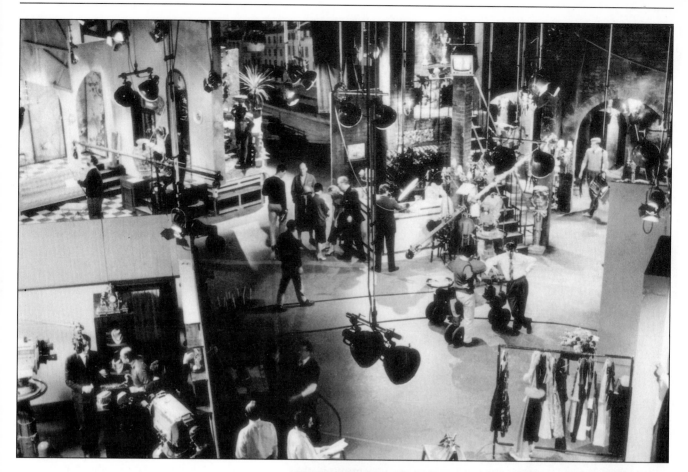

Jack Warner, Kathleen Harrison and Flora Robson, and done straight dramatic parts in several of the ATV series made by Lew (now Lord) Grade in the early days of independent television. He kept trying to give me line readings to start with. I couldn't say a comedy line to save my life, so he eventually gave up.

"Do you know, Patrick, the way that you do it is the way it *should* be done," he said. "At least it's right for *you*. It's not right for anyone else, but for you it is." This is, I suppose, the dichotomy of me, with my soft eyes, doing a show that *required* a sort of 'I'll grab you now or else I'll miss you and you'll all turn off' type delivery.

In New York, John Frankenheimer would follow you around — as did Peter Hammond — *very* closely with a viewfinder. They would look at you through the viewfinder to see how you would appear on screen. The reason they did this was because live, or 'as-live' taped television, was based entirely on the close-up. The close-up in television was vital, because the screen in those days was so small. So if your face came on and you were at a distance, say in a field of poppies, it was no good, it didn't make any statement at all. It had to be *you* saying, "I love you," or, "Get the hell off my turf!" or whatever. And it had to be with blazing eyes and in close-up.

I had been acting in live TV shows one after

Sans bowler hat and suit as a fairground barker in 'The Tunnel of Fear'.

the other, so it didn't phase me. I was prepared and on my spot, and knew that my little moment before the camera would come and I had to be ready. You couldn't be talking to somebody, you had to be on the ball. David Greene always used to say to us, before our productions in Toronto, "*Total* concentration for the next two hours... I mean *total* concentration." Most people don't know what concentration means. When that little red light shows on the camera, you know that it's on *you*, and when it's not, that you've got to be ready for when it is again — and yet you've also got to relate to the person who is being filmed by the other camera. The other actor would have their own camera, and we flipped from close-up to close-up to close-up and the concentration on one's partner in the piece was total — it had to be total.

By 1964 it was a film camera, of course, which was used with remarkable facility by Sidney Hayers, Roy Baker, James Hill, Charlie Crichton, Peter Graham Scott and other hugely talented directors, all of whom were very experienced film men and had worked for the producer Julian Wintle before. Working on live television and filmed television calls for two completely different techniques, but they are still for the *camera*.

Giving a performance before the camera is easier said than done. You have to blank out

almost the rest of life, because the constant energy required is immeasurable. You have to have good health. You have to have tremendous stamina — a stamina that requires you to have good manners and be pleasant and gracious to the huge number of actors and technical people one works with.

Day after day Ian and I would do this. I was having a gorgeous time working on the series, in which, though I say so myself, I was acting really well (but hardly knew it at the time). I was working with all sorts of people, as well as this towering genius, Ian Hendry, a man exuding talent and wonderful, highly original creativity.

———

Ian had a great interest in theatre and the circus. He had worked in the Big Top for a time and had developed a very close friendship with Coco the Clown.

In fact, now that I think of it, the only episode that I never worked on was the one about the circus, 'Girl on the Trapeze', written by Dennis Spooner. Ian didn't want me in that. He just wanted to do it his way — the *right* way. All his love and experience of the sawdust ring went into that. It was a masterful piece of work.

Ian had a trick he would perform, presumably taught to him by Coco. Whenever a party was flagging, he would sit on something — a grand piano perhaps, a window ledge, or a public bar — and he'd fall head first towards the ground, do a flip in mid air and land on his feet! It was spectacular to watch. (He didn't always get it right, of course! But nine times out of ten he would perform it to perfection.)

Teddington was a hive of activity, back then. There was never a dull moment, and the studio provided us with lots of light relief. Sydney Newman was a lovely man and had the respect of everyone around him, but no one ever had a discussion with Sydney. He just shouted at you.

I remember one time when Ted Kotcheff, a very famous director, was fed up with being shouted at and threatened to throw Sydney out of his office window on the fourth floor. He literally held him outside the window and said, "I'm going to drop you unless..." Sydney was reputed to have said, as Ted, towering with rage, lifted him back inside his office to safety, "And another thing, Ted..." Sydney always had the last word.

There was another director called Dennis Vance, a witty and volatile man who directed many of the first *Armchair Theatre* shows for Sydney Newman, not to mention Ian and myself in the first season story called 'Please Don't Feed the Animals'.

Some time during the summer of 1961, when Ian and I were doing well with the series, we popped into The Anglers. We'd been there for several minutes when Dennis Vance came crashing in with a carving knife in his hand.

"Where is she?" he growled. "Where is she?"

"Where is who?" we asked.

It turned out that he was having a fling with his personal assistant. He told us her name. We said we hadn't seen her.

"Yes you bloody well have!" he roared, as several people edged away from our table. We shook our heads. We hadn't seen her. What was he going to do?

"I'm going to bloody kill her!" he shouted, his eyes circling the room. We laughed at this and he thundered out of the door.

He didn't kill her, of course, but we learned later that he had stormed into her office and raced around with the carving knife, scaring her associates half to death. At the same moment, the coffee lady came by, pushing her trolley, which was piled up with cups and saucers and a huge coffee urn. As she turned to enter the office, Vance spotted his girlfriend standing behind her. Knocking the startled coffee lady aside, he lunged through the door, reached out with the knife and nicked the girl in the cheek.

He didn't do her any great harm, but they took him into custody and he spent some time in jail for assault. I don't know how long he served, but he was back at work in a couple of weeks.

———

After we'd been doing the show for about six

months, we discovered that we must have been doing something right, because it was decided to extend the production right through to thirty-nine episodes. We were successful and I was loving every minute of it.

As was **Sydney Newman**. What I didn't know, until now, is why Sydney never took a credit for creating the show:

'After conceiving the series I only concerned myself with helping Leonard set up the first few episodes — as head of the department I had other fish to fry. I merely kept a benign eye on it, revelling in its success.

'In retrospect, it's too bad that I did not give myself a credit on the end titles as devisor of *The Avengers*. I did not because, unlike Britain or the USA, in Canada heads of departments did not give themselves a credit. I made the same stupid mistake at the BBC where I created *Doctor Who*. Considering their international success, the royalties from those two programmes would have made me a somewhat more financially secure person than I am today. Oh well, *c'est la vie*.'

Things were moving along favourably. Then, in October 1961, our union, British Actors' Equity Association, decided that we had to strike against the Independent Television Company!! ■

A dramatic scene from 'Double Danger'. (Seated left to right: Ron Pember, Vanda Hudson, Peter Reynolds.)

Imagine my concern. Having worked for nine months with Ian Hendry, and convinced myself that I was about to start living at long last, after the rag-taggle, pillar-to-post type of life I'd led, there we were in the winter of 1961 and we had nothing... *I* had nothing. My short brush with success was about to be abruptly terminated. I felt wretched.

The dispute was between the British Actors' Equity Association and Independent Television. Before the birth of ITV in 1955, acting on television — BBC Television — had been accepted as an extension of straight theatre work or film work. When ITV came into being the situation changed. Viewing figures (ratings) became a consideration. As programmes began to reach a larger audience, the ITV companies saw their profits increase dramatically and Equity decided that its membership should receive a bigger slice of the cake.

In layman's terms, they were demanding an increase in the minimum fee paid to artistes for programmes seen on the network, additional increases for shows that were partially networked and a much higher rehearsal fee. The dispute actually only affected about ten per cent of Equity's membership, those who were deemed to be earning their living mainly from TV, but the rallying call was also supported by the remaining ninety per cent of members.

Television didn't mean *anything* in the early days of broadcasting. Between 1947 and 1960 we just sort of battered along. People didn't consider that they were really working when they did television. The rehearsals were long, the results haphazard and the pay laughable.

I remember acting in the O'Neill play *Long Day's Journey Into Night* with Beatrix Lehmann. Kenneth Tynan, the famous English theatre critic, author and devisor of the nude revue *Oh Calcutta!*, was the assistant director. I remember saying to him, "About my performance..." He said, "Don't worry about your performance — the wallpaper's lovely!" Television was not remotely serious in those days, it was simply the poor relation of the theatre. Years before, I had done several television plays from Alexandra Palace, but what one earned was, literally, slave pay. Indeed, if anyone asked, "Are you working?" We used to say, "No. We're doing television!" It was right to have the strike, because after all it enabled actors to hit back.

I sympathised with Equity's actions, but the threatened lay-off left me wondering, "Where do I go from here?" The thought of insecurity terrified me.

They kept me idle for five months during the strike. I didn't do anything, except get myself an agent, Richard Hatton, who put me into the BBC TV production of the Shakespeare play *The Winter's Tale* with Robert Shaw. Shaw played Leontes. I played Polixenes.

We rehearsed in an old schoolroom down in Wandsworth and one day found ourselves next door to each other, having a pee in the outhouse urinal. Shaw turned to me and asked would I like to be in a play by Harold Pinter?

Startled, I replied, "Yes."

He said, "Harold will phone you tonight."

Harold Pinter phoned, and offered me a nice part in his new play, *The Collector*, which was coming on at The Aldwych in a month or two. Obviously, I was flattered. However, the strike ended in May 1962 and I went back to work on *The Avengers*.

———

But Ian Hendry had gone! Ian, the incredible magnet of our show, the *inspiration*, the man who daily pushed in to me what I should be trying to get out of the show... which, I must say, strangely enough turned me into a series participator. And quite unique and original I was by this time. I'd got the smart clothes. I had

LEATHER

Above: Guns were customary in the first season, of course. But, thereafter, when appropriate, I spurned firearms in favour of the umbrella.

Right: What's that I said about guns? Well, of course, this is a publicity picture.

acquired the bowler hat and the umbrella, but I never *carried* a gun! I'd served five years in the Second World War, in the Navy, and had seen enough of guns. Steed carried an umbrella.

"An *umbrella*!" they exclaimed.

"*Yes*," I told them, "but what wonderful devices there are going to be in that umbrella!" (In retrospect, I'm so pleased I did that, because in the politically correct nineties, to see me come in with a bowler hat and umbrella shows a tremendous amount of cool. I don't have to hide behind a gun. I'm proud of that.)

So Steed was a *character*. I, however, had done very little work and had got through my savings. I had very little left.

I let this slip to Marie Donaldson, the ABC Television public relations lady, who was great and thought up all sorts of publicity to promote the show. She assured me that the company would give me an advance against my salary. I presume she must have mentioned this to ABPC, the parent company of ABC. A couple of days later, I was told that Howard Thomas had authorised the payment. They had granted me a retainer of £50 a week: a cheque for £200, four weeks' advance, would be mailed to my agent during the next couple of days.

A letter from the ABPC financial adviser dropped through my letterbox shortly afterwards. Unambiguous, it advised that while the company was pleased to confirm that the payment I'd requested had been forwarded to my agent, the company wished to make it quite clear that it would not entertain a further request!

Borrowing the money was my first big, dreadful mistake. I never should have done it. I should have borrowed from other sources, because forever after that they had a hold on me. They used to tell me later, "You're good for us, Pat. You're a company man, had experience as a CEO. Oh yes, you'll get on with us, Pat." I paid it back, of course, as soon as I could, but they never let me forget it!

I remember that after the strike, ABPC's Head of Finance called me into his office.

"You think you've won, Macnee," he growled. "You've had a five month strike and you think that you've won. Well, not with us you haven't! John Paul was sacked from *Probation Officer*. You are getting an extra £5 a week. That's £155 a week, not a penny more!"

I accepted this and returned to work, concerned that things wouldn't be the same now that Ian had left us to pursue a career in cinema.

Sydney Newman recalls the circumstances that led to Ian's departure:

'My baby had been alive and running for twenty-six weeks when we were forced to a halt on 30 December 1961 because of the

strike which hit commercial television. As the scripts began piling up waiting for the strike to end, the series suffered a devastating blow. Ian Hendry had become so popular that his talents were recognised by the film industry. Apologetically he asked to be released from the series because he couldn't refuse a firm, multi-picture movie contract, which would pay more money than television could. That's showbiz, with a vengeance.'

It was fifteen years before I saw Ian Hendry again. He joined us as a guest star in *The New Avengers* episode 'To Catch a Rat'.

It was extraordinary getting together with Ian again after all those years. He'd changed, of course. We all do. By then he was no longer playing the big parts. But he'd done so much in his career — big, important, *vital* parts in television, on stage and in movies. His talent was enormous, and he still had power as an actor when he did this episode. In 'To Catch a Rat', when I said, "Seventeen years too late," I meant every word. The scenes between Ian and Edward Judd are not just everyday acting. It is really good, so tremendously strong and powerful.

I saw Ian again two years later, this time to celebrate his *This is Your Life* tribute (transmitted 15 February 1978). The presenter, Eamonn Andrews, and myself sprang the surprise on Ian from the Sheraton Park Hotel in London. Hidden from sight in the hotel's roof-garden, we must have looked a very odd couple indeed, me dressed in the clothes I had worn

during *The New Avengers* some nine months earlier, Eamonn dressed in identical attire. I remember Eamonn saying that he hoped we would "arrest Ian in his tracks."

He needn't have worried. At that moment, Ian was making his way across the hotel's forecourt in the belief that he was there to do an interview with a Sunday newspaper columnist. He had no idea of what was about to take place. The recipients of the Big Red Book never do, the surprise element being an integral part of the show's format. Take my word for it, the look of astonishment — terror? — on the subject's face is *real*...

...As was the look on Ian's face when Eamonn approached him seconds before he entered the hotel.

"Your old sparring partner, Patrick Macnee, has flown 6,000 miles to be with you tonight," said Eamonn, brandishing the red leather volume under Ian's nose as I crept up behind him. He turned. The look on his face said it all.

"How are you, darling," he grinned. "It's incredible, Pat... just incredible!" he chortled, as the three of us walked to the limousine that would take us to the Thames Television studio. "It's mad," he said cheerfully as Steed-lookalike Eamonn climbed in beside us, "You look like two bookends!"

———

With no Ian Hendry, the second season of *The Avengers* began with another actor playing the doctor character — Jon Rollason, a sweet man. We played three shows together, then

Steed persuades Cathy to stand as a Parliamentary candidate to investigate political corruption and the theft of a nuclear warhead! (From 'November Five'.)

Jon disappeared!

Nothing was said to me about why he'd left, but the producers must have been planning and plotting, because suddenly Sydney Newman, with that remarkable instinct he had, said let's have a woman.

I guess that they thought of a woman as being better able to partner me, this rather strange, old-fashioned man who dressed in sort of pansy clothes, because without Ian Hendry I was... well, a bit lost. With Ian gone, they pretended *I* was such a success that they felt I — *Steed* — should carry on in a central sense. The thought of my working alone seemingly hadn't occurred to them. Well of course, I couldn't have done, because I could never act on my own. I simply haven't got the personality to be able to say, "I'm me", like Sean Connery or Peter O'Toole can. I'm not a *star*. I'm a man. My agent first said to me, "You have a great face, Pat, but no mouth." I know what he meant. I'm like Kenneth Branagh, without the rest of it... I'm not a classical actor, that level is too much for me. I have played classical parts, of course. Richard Hatton said I

could have had a career in it. I don't think so... but then as Diana Rigg always said to me, "Patrick, you're your own worst enemy. You have no faith in yourself and consequently you're not half as good as you could be."

Suddenly, perhaps because I seemed to play and represent the character of Steed so truthfully to myself, I became what was representative of the sort of England that had passed. I had a certain dignity, a certain flair and a certain hopefulness that was based on the conventions of the so called English 'stiff-upper-lip' — a convention that people understood. This was then sent up when the women came on the scene and they always called me Steed, while I called them *Mrs* Gale, *Mrs* Peel, *Miss* King.

Also, because as a boy I grew up entirely surrounded by women, one assumed that the women would take the reins and tell me what to do, which was entirely right for Steed. Not that Steed was effete or homosexual or ineffective. I was quite strong both in gait and general energy. I lived for the moment and I lived for the past, but I couldn't think ahead. So consequently I was ideal for this role of a man who just sort of slithered through life. I *was* Steed.

During the first season, the power of Ian Hendry carried us through, but I didn't really know what I was doing there except following his lead. When you get into that sort of 'follow the leader' type of thing, you accept what other people tell you. Like Sydney Newman saying, "Right, we're going to have a woman in the show." Of course it was right to have a woman in the show, but I was still as much of a male chauvinist as anybody else.

They came up with Mrs Catherine Gale.

Sydney Newman illuminates the circumstances surrounding his make-or-break decision:

'The series' format was too good to throw away, but after weeks of considering many actors, Leonard and I could not find anyone we liked to fill Hendry's shoes. But adversity can be a spur, if exploited.

'One night, watching the news on television, I saw an item dealing with the Mau Mau terrorists in Kenya which absolutely shattered me. I was powerfully moved by a woman settler calmly telling the TV reporter of a frightful occurrence. When she was cooking dinner she heard terrible screams coming from the rest of the house. As she turned to find out what it was, three terrorist Mau Mau with machetes dripping blood fled past her and ran out of the kitchen. She rushed into the living room to face the horrible sight of her two young sons and husband dead, the latter decapitated.

'What knocked me out was the woman. She was a well-set, once pretty woman of about forty wearing slacks and a bush jacket. On her

Producer Leonard White's choice for my new partner, Honor Blackman. Her impact on viewers was astounding.

back was her baby in a papoose-like bag, but strapped around her waist was a bullet-studded belt with an enormous pistol in a holster. A baby beside a pistol! She and her husband had come out from England years back to farm, and she explained that the terrorist attacks were so common that all settler's wives carried guns and knew how to use them. That woman was beyond my imagination. Unforgettable! She gave me the answer to the Hendry casting problem.

'Why shouldn't Hendry's role be played by a woman, I thought. God knows, women were, in life, doing incredible things: Margaret Bourke-White, internationally famous *Life* photographer who covered wars; Margaret Mead, the anthropologist; and my most competent wife, Betty. A woman actively physical, attractive and demonstrating intelligence would certainly be fresh and different. Now, thinking about it, it was years ahead of the women's lib movement as recognised by the media today.

'The next morning I dictated a memo to Leonard saying that I felt that a *woman*, but with the same characteristics as Hendry's — physical *and* brainy — should be found, to be Macnee's opposite in every way. I described how Steed would find her working as an anthropologist at the British Museum after her husband and children had been killed by the Mau Mau in Kenya. As was the case with most settler's wives, for protection she was proficient at using weapons and prepared to fight. She should be in her early thirties and attractive. She would be primly disapproving of Macnee's amorality and Macnee would always be wanting to bed her and never succeed. With the exception of the sex angle, the chemistry of the two characters was to be the same as the old *Avengers*. The new sex element would give the series a zest it never had before.

'In such a case it was important to get the producer's wholehearted agreement, and that I got from Leonard. I had an actress in mind to play the woman — Nyree Dawn Porter, who had been superb as the mannequin come to life in 'His Polyvinyl Girl', my musical drama *Armchair Theatre*. Just before I was to go off on a three week family holiday, Leonard White, as producer, brought to me a shortlist of proposed actresses for approval to replace Hendry. Sure enough, Nyree's name was on it, but so was Leonard's choice, the lovely Honor Blackman.

'"No Leonard," I cried out. "I can't stand Blackman's perpetual, Rank-starlet trained, say-everything-with-a-smile, kind of acting. She's

Warlock

Recorded as part of the pilot episode for the second season, the following sequences served to introduce Cathy Gale, although they were rewritten and refilmed to acknowledge the fact that Steed and Mrs Gale were already familiar to each other (and to viewers) courtesy of a couple of shows televised prior to this episode being broadcast. What follows is the original script.

'Warlock' (Episode #31, by Doreen Montgomery).

Investigating the mental breakdown of Neville, a scientist working on a secret government research project, Steed finds the man clutching a feather smeared with dried blood and a needle through its spine. In the man's belongings Steed finds other items: several brochures and books on psychic research and spiritualism, and a large black book with a pentacle design on its cover, *The Black Art* — an occult Grimoire.

Disturbed that Neville is dabbling in the occult, One-Ten arranges for Steed to seek expert advice from a specialist working at the British Museum — Mrs Catherine Gale.

INT. STUDIO. FOSSIL ROOM. MUSEUM. DAY.
A TEMPORARILY SHUT-OFF ROOM OF THE MUSEUM — GLASS CASES CONTAINING SPECIMENS. A MAMMOTH SKELETON, MAYBE A RECONSTRUCTION OF A DINOSAUR. CATHY GALE IS WORKING AT A TABLE. SHE LOOKS UP.
CATHY: Mr Steed? Do come and sit down.
STEED (SURPRISED): Mrs Gale?
CATHY: Yes.
STEED: I'm sorry — it's just that I didn't expect to find you so attractive.
CATHY: Just because you have to meet me at the British Museum you expect tweeds and glasses. Isn't that a bit old-fashioned of you, Mr Steed?
STEED: Perhaps, but I find it a relief in this fast-moving world.
CATHY: I was told that you wanted some information about Black Magic practices.
STEED: Yes. (HANDS HER HEX FEATHER.) I think this is called a hex symbol.

Hereafter, with minor changes, the dialogue/action remains faithful to the televised version.

The tag scene, however, was totally rewritten from this, the original version.

INT. STUDIO. COVENT GARDEN PUB. NIGHT.
BARMAID BRINGS DRINK TO ONE-TEN WHO PAYS.
BARMAID: Thank you, sir.
ONE-TEN: Have you any crisps?
BARMAID: Yes, sir.
ONE-TEN: I'll have a packet.
BARMAID PRODUCES THEM. ONE-TEN OPENS PACKET. STARTS TO EAT. BARMAID BRINGS CHANGE.
ONE-TEN: Thank you.
HE EATS ANOTHER CRISP THEN TURNS AS STEED AND CATHY ENTER.
ONE-TEN (TO STEED): You're late!
STEED: I'm sorry. (TO CATHY) I'd like you to meet...
ONE-TEN (SMILES): Hello, Cathy. Half a bitter as usual?
CATHY: Please.
ONE-TEN TURNS TO BARMAID.
STEED (TO CATHY): Is this where you get your laugh?
CATHY: That's right. (BEAT) One-Ten wanted a *woman* used on this one. We knew you'd hate to work with a woman, so I didn't give you a chance to say no.
STEED: I should have been told.
CATHY: Well, you did try to find out, didn't you?
STEED (SMILES): You keep your secrets very well.
CATHY: No better than any other *woman*.
STEED: That stuff about you being a widow? Was that true?
CATHY: Oh yes... there were one or two things I *wanted* you to know.
ONE-TEN (RETURNS WITH DRINKS): Cheers.
CATHY/STEED: Cheers.
ONE-TEN: We've identified the dead man as Sergie Ilyich Markel. He's been on our list for some time. The other thing is the verdict on Cosmo Gallion. Coronary thrombosis — just like Peter Neville. (TO CATHY) He must have got quite a shock when he saw that you were immune to his... power.
STEED (TO ONE-TEN): It was a clever trick.
ONE-TEN: Yes. You should get on well together.

FADE TO BLACK. F/U SLIDE F/U GRAMS.
Theme music. ■

Opposite above: The man getting his just desserts is actor Geoff L'Cise. (From 'Death Dispatch'.)

Opposite below: A practice session in the gym. The man going over my head is Doug Robinson.

wrong for the part. Go for Nyree Dawn Porter. Right?" Loyal as ever, Leonard said, "Right."

'When I returned from holiday, I blew my top when Leonard told me that he had signed Honor Blackman as Mrs Cathy Gale. Somewhat gracelessly I accepted his explanation that Nyree was unavailable — she was in a West End play — and none of the others on the list were available either. I had to hold my breath and wait for the pilot film to see how wrong Leonard was. Seeing it, there were, I had to admit, signs of an exciting chemistry between Honor and Patrick upon which the series depended. I could see too that her presence sure perked Pat up.

'The pilot production was well worth the money it cost. The chemistry was there — and that (ugh!) smile — but dammit, she did look lovely despite her short-bobbed hair, which I loathed. "Okay," I said to Leonard, "we'll go with her, but with these provisos. Don't ever let her smile." This was an outrageous thing to ask, but Leonard read me well with his usual forbearance. I repeated that she was only to accept Steed and not *like* him and, specifically, get rid of her cutesy bobbed hair. "Get her a shoulder length wig until her own hair grows long."'

I certainly didn't really appreciate Honor when she arrived. I thought, "You're beautiful. You've got enormous bosoms and a strikingly beautiful face, but I remember you when you were just a typical English rose."

Honor came in and was a dear, sweet, relaxed lady whose sheer beauty, control and poise had taken her to the top of her profession in the movies. She was an experienced, talented actress.

By this time, I had a small mews flat in South Kensington. I invited Honor to come round and see me, and decided to be Ian Hendry to her Patrick Macnee. I got on my high horse and told her that *The Avengers* wasn't just a cops and robbers television show, it had something *more*. It had depth. It had urgency. It was *original*.

Looking straight into my eyes (as she would do at all times, without being domineering), she inclined her head, fixed me with a steely-eyed look of indifference and sighed. Her demeanour said it all. She *knew* what was required of her.

So we threw ourselves into it and went from there.

———

Honor, of course, was required to throw herself into it in more ways than one; unlike Steed, the scripts required her to fight off the villains with judo. The action scenes worried her. She didn't know how to fight.

"Patrick," she said. "I'm a woman. I don't

Honor, previously known as a typical English Rose, became a rose that grew thorns.

know anything about guns or knives."

Leonard White wanted her to do judo. "In that case," said Honor, "you'll have to teach me."

The judo idea was dropped for a couple of shows or so. By then the scriptwriters could think of nothing better than to suggest that Cathy went for 'the gun in her handbag' — a ludicrous situation really, as by the time she'd found the gun and taken the safety-catch off, she'd have been dead. Honor asked if anyone in the cast knew anything about judo. One did. An actor-stuntman called Geoff L'Cise knew a couple of moves. He showed Honor how to throw a man and she took it from there. Honor looked so good that the scriptwriters latched on and started to write fights into the script. Some time later Honor went off to judo classes with Doug and Joe Robinson.

As we were to discover, there's a problem with throwing people about, particularly when you're a woman. Your pants have a tendency to split, leaving one's posterior on view to the casual observer.

During rehearsal for one of the first episodes, Honor was meant to heave this brute of a man out of her way. She was wearing trousers at the time. She tackled the man, and her trousers split down the middle, while her backside was facing the camera! Well, we couldn't have that happening to our heroine.

Something tough and durable was required. I suggested suede. Leonard White said, "That's no good, it absorbs light... but what about the other side. What about leather?"

At least that's how I remember it.

Sydney Newman tells a different story, and he should know:

'Other flaws were revealed in the pilot. Because the show was being shot live, no stunt doubles could be used. Leonard had made sure that Honor was given judo lessons which she took to eagerly. Also in the pilot, in vanquishing a villain, a real problem was seen. When she took a backward leap, her skirt flew up revealing her brief underpants. Can't have that — no, not in 1962! Her dress tore as well, revealing a handsome set of bra'd breasts. We decided that a special wardrobe would be designed for her to eliminate both cleavages, legs and bosom, which might offend the sensibilities of the ITA (and the few burgeoning Mary Whitehouses of the nation). Our costume lady knew that next autumn leather would be the vogue attire and so Honor was fitted out with culottes, slit skirts, tight long pants and tight tops, all in shiny leather.'

Leather was the most practical gear for Honor, because it held tight and didn't split when she

Leather was the most practical gear for Honor, because it held tight and didn't split.

did these violent physical things.

At first no one realised the importance of the idea and the studio technicians disliked it because black wouldn't televise. So the first leather outfit had to be green. When lighting techniques improved, Honor wore jet black leather all the time, which gave a charge to people, particularly when they saw it on Honor's soft, female frame. Lit and oiled, it can be a second skin, and hugely erotic. At the time it was seen as something frightfully naughty. We knew that, of course. I like to think that we went for it *because* it was a fetish. We used bondage... we *suggested* bondage. We implied everything on that show, but mainly we used humour. Without humour none of it would have worked.

Incidentally, the 'pilot' episode referred to by Syd Newman was 'Warlock'.

Scriptwriter **Roger Marshall** joined the team early in the second season. Five years later he was still writing many of the best scripts. No one is better qualified to express an opinion on the merits — or otherwise — of the video-taped shows:

'Doreen Montgomery invited me to write for the show. It was she who christened 'Cathy Gale' and issued a directive that her part should be written exactly as if it were a man's.

'It seems amazing now, but my first reaction was to pass on it. Family, friends, even my agent counselled caution. Could my fragile career survive something as dreadful as *The Avengers*? I'm talking, of course, of the pre-Cathy Gale era. It was mind-blowingly, jaw-achingly dreadful. In today's harsher climate it wouldn't have survived six weeks. The central scheduler would have sent for a hearse. It would have gone, unlamented, to its grave before Steed ever put on his first bowler or twiddled his first brolly. A mere 150-odd episodes short of its final total.

'Don Leaver tells stories of how rehearsals began with Ian Hendry dropping the new script in the waste bin and saying, "Right. What's this one going to be about?" No wonder the viewers couldn't follow it. Apart from directors like Don Leaver and Peter Hammond, the only plus marks visible were the Dankworth title music and the sets. However nonsensical the plot, it usually looked good — shows made at Teddington always devoted more of their budget to design than any other company's. A strong visual sense was the hallmark of the studio that nurtured Saville, Kotcheff and Jarrott.

'Being cynical, I wrote my first two episodes in collaboration, on the premise that a credit shared was blame halved. What changed my mind? 'Death of a Great Dane' and Peter Hammond. For the first time I met a director who could take a script and turn it into an experience way beyond one's wildest expectations. I was hooked.'

Roger's opinion mirrors my own. Way ahead of his time, Peter Hammond managed to bring a novel 'look' to the videotaped shows and single-handedly set the series' style. The following illustrates this so well. I'm delighted to include this transcript of comments by **Harry Craig** from *The Critics*, a programme broadcast on BBC Radio in 1963, as a personal tribute to Peter's talents. Harry's talking about the episode 'Conspiracy of Silence':

'*The Avengers* is a thriller that, to make no bones about it, is as empty as a dry skull. Do I praise it too much? Because as I am always reluctant to put a skull back on the ground, I am never impatient to get to the end of *The Avengers* when Peter Hammond is directing it. For to me, it's impossible to watch this stupidity, this excellent stupidity, this silly excellence without being struck by black thoughts about design and vision, about content and about form. You see, it is made brilliantly. There are shots in it, passages in it, that suggests the time set up to re-take and editing [found] in good cinema. There are sideways tracking shots from one set to another that succeed. There is

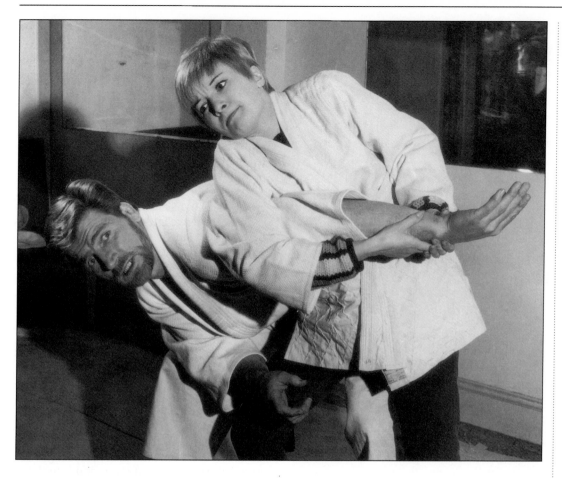

Julie Stevens gets tough with stunt-man/actor Joe Robinson.

a use of shadow... of photographing in shadow... that dares to and *does* it.

'Let me describe one shot last Sunday. The heroine, the beautiful Honor Blackman, is in big close-up, sitting; the hero, the Edwardian gent Patrick Macnee, sits in a rocking chair beside her, and as he talks he rocks in and out, his face in big close-up across her big close-up face. Effective? Of course it's effective... The excitement of *The Avengers*, its image, its imagination, has a mark to it that I suppose is the Sydney Newman stamp. When I saw *The Avengers* first it was also directed by Peter Hammond, and his work had made me jump as it did here, in this story about a circus.

'On a few square yards of studio floor he spun around and dizzied us into the atmosphere of a circus. *The Avengers* is an example of commercial art and it's certainly interesting to see how sophisticated commercial art can be served up to a popular audience. But there is never any danger of confusing commercial art with real art, is there? The commercial opens the eye, but in real television art the visual excitement works with the narrative to deepen, to signify, to intensify. *The Avengers* is excited surface.

'What is it about? Search me! It has the usual vocabulary of a thriller, gun play and judo throw, with a hero who goes through imminent deadly ambush with a bowler hat and rolled umbrella, a nostalgic return to Lord Peter Wimsey. But 'bah!' to the goose of *The Avengers'* stories. The visual image is not used to heighten the story — it is almost a story — it takes over...

'When I first saw *The Avengers*, Peter Hammond was directing it and I spent the next day going around asking people. "Who was this person? What work had he done before? What age was he?" All the questions that one asks, and it was afterwards that I began to wonder what this work might be doing to an artist. Peter Hammond is an artist of this calibre.'

The enormity of getting the series going again made for a terrifying time. It was thought that I needed a contrast to this self-assured, controlled woman and someone, Howard Thomas I think, suggested having a jazz singer type, the idea being to alternate Steed's partners on a weekly basis.

Julie Stevens was selected to play nightclub singer Venus Smith:

'ABC phoned me one morning to ask if I could go down to the studio. Leonard White and Don Leaver were there. We talked about this role in *The Avengers*. I read a bit, sang a bit — and I remember Don Leaver telling Leonard, "I don't think she can do it." I've no idea whether he was referring to my acting ability,

Sydney Newman: "Honor and Patrick produced sparks. She beautiful, agile and full of integrity, and Pat, the lascivious dandy, the whimsical, but efficient killer on behalf of his country."

whether I could sing and be convincing or what, but they asked me back to Teddington that night. Dave Lee was there at the piano. I sang and they said that I should be at rehearsals the next morning. It was as simple as that!

'I'll never forget my first day with Dave Lee and the boys. We wanted to get this thing working, because they wanted a sort of sophisticated jazz feel to the songs. After several false starts, I asked Dave if he could help me with the backing, by injecting more swing into the vocals. Tinkling the keyboard, he looked at me and said, "Julie, sweetheart. If you went to New Orleans now, slept with every musician, drank yourself into the ground and sung your head off, you could *never* learn to swing!" — which hardly boosted one's confidence! He told me that *they* could move it along, "but don't expect too much of yourself, because it's

not in your genes, love. It's not in your *soul*!" And he was right. I was just a very ordinary girl from Manchester who used to listen to Elvis. It didn't seem to bother them that I had no singing experience at all!

'I really enjoyed the first two shows that I did, in which I played a sophisticated night-club singer, decked out in long, figure-hugging ballroom dresses. I wore a wig in those. Then they sent me to Vidal Sassoon, who was just starting his 'boy' haircut look. He cropped my hair, bleached it blonde, and it looked as though I'd got no hair at all, but it did look good on the screen. Then, after a long gap, they started putting me into these teenage things, like the French postman's hat, sweaters, jeans and boots, which I thought were hideous and made me look like an idiot child.

'By that time, Honor had become this huge whirlwind. So when it came time for them to take up the option on my contract, I didn't even consider asking anybody if they'd let me stay, because her character was so good, so strong. I had no complaints whatsoever with their decision to part with me.'

What they hadn't considered, I soon realised, was that instead of doing one episode every ten days, I, because I was in both, now had to rehearse two episodes simultaneously. I would race from one rehearsal room to another, rehearse a bit for the episode with Julie, then scamper back upstairs to pick up where I'd left off on the show I was doing with Honor.

A word about this to Leonard White instigated a memo to Sydney Newman:

'As the situation stands at the moment, several factors make it imperative that we plan to record episodes on a *fortnightly* basis. Scripting for the new character format is on the basis of dual leads in each episode, and I don't think it would be wise to introduce 'Cathy only' scripts into the series too soon. The Steed character is bound to carry a great weight for some while and I, quite frankly, don't think that Patrick Macnee will stand up to the pressures of a turn-round less than fortnightly.'

I *knew* that I couldn't stand up to the pressure. Each day at the studio was just sheer hard slog — grinding, grinding work. It became less so when they decided that Honor and I were the team and I no longer had to learn and perform two episodes a week.

That's when Honor and I became magically bonded. We started doing things in the show that we would never have had the guts to do unless we had this tremendous rapport, this man/woman relationship, which really worked very well indeed. Using our own egos, we pushed it hard and turned out a show that seemingly entranced people. We were ahead of our time.

But then so was the Pat McGoohan show, *Danger Man* (known as *Secret Agent* in the US), which was in many ways better, because it was made on film... and yet he never quite got the glamour that we had, because we had the ineffable advantage of having a woman as a lead character.

The point being that getting on with a woman is something that very few people did. *The Avengers* had an extraordinary ability, without Honor being too butch or me being too effete, to make a relationship between two people with different genital organs *communicate*. Not in a married sense, not in a 'lovers' sense, but in an androgynous sense... well, not even androgynous, because one did feel that after the episode ended they stripped off the leather and dandy clothes and got down to a little indulgent lovemaking. (At least I like to think so!)

Honor, previously known as a typical English Rose, became a rose that grew thorns, which is what shook the programme right up into the first league and made Honor a sort of icon. This beautiful blonde bombshell in the black leather breeches was suddenly doing something that no other woman had done on television before. She was a woman being equal, exciting, beautiful and special. Cathy Gale had become a symbol of the jet-age woman. (This was a glorious accident, of course. We didn't know that feminism was coming in, the decision just happened to coincide with the time when women began to make a stand for equality and equal pay in the work place.)

As **Sydney Newman** recounts, we had become a team:

'It didn't take weeks before *The Avengers* took the public by storm. Honor and Patrick produced sparks; she beautiful, agile and full of integrity, and Pat, the lascivious dandy, the whimsical but efficient killer on behalf of his country.

'How Leonard, as its producer, and the actors and staff took that weekly grind evoked my fullest admiration. It was his leadership and his production team that made it work.

'Its two main directors, Peter Hammond and Don Leaver, met an impossible schedule by weekly leap-frogging each other with camera work that was tight, handsome and cut fast. The designers had a ball! There were times when Pat and Honor would demand to see me to complain about the scripts. I would pour oil on them to keep them going. John Bryce and Pat Brawn, the story editors, had the task of getting script after script filled with action and throwaway wit, but Bryce, not unhappily, confessed that a lot of the humour was created in the rehearsal room by Pat and Honor,

with the connivance of the two directors and the final support of Leonard.

'Patrick, as I knew he would be, was always professionally rock-solid no matter what the crisis, disgustingly handsome, and supportive of the beautiful and equally professional Honor. There was never any sense of competition for the limelight, they simply enjoyed acting together.'

The show aired on ITV, and the critics loved us:

'*The Avengers* were originally a couple of hombres who shared the perils in alternate segments,' wrote *Variety*. 'Now John Steed (Patrick Macnee — a fund of insolence and reckless good looks) is joined by femme agent Catherine Gale (Honor Blackman — cucumber cool, provocatively clad), and the coupling had quite an edge in this opener. As Macnee plays

Honor displays her Dillinger pistol 'garter gun' to good effect in 'The Outside-In Man'.

Right: Steed would often gain Cathy's interest in an oblique way — usually during casual conversation.

Opposite above: Honor, showing courage beyond the call of duty.

Opposite below: During camera rehearsals for the videotaped shows.

him, Steed is a positive and eye-catching figure, although he seems inclined to overdo the nonchalant imprudence. The hinted romantic undertones with Cathy gave extra bite.'

'In the name of all that is defiantly British, I urge you to watch *The Avengers*,' advised an Australian newspaper critic when the series began showing Down Under, plaudits dripping from his keyboard. 'Its hero is chipper secret service chappie John Steed, a master of the art of one-upmanship. While the dumb cops fuss over a dead man, Steed takes one look at his eyes and instantly observes — "He's been poisoned by something in the hexa-bar-bitone group!" His girl Friday is earthy, brunette (*sic*) Cathy Gale — a judo expert who keeps a pistol tucked in her garter! Her favourite on-camera fashions include black lace underwear and knee-high leather boots. I kid you not.

'Catherine's hobby is fighting!

'She whams baddies senseless with one wallop of her delicate little fist. If that fails, she has a powder compact that shoots bullets! And, by gad, if a lady like that doesn't stir up your sporting tee-vee blood, chaps, nothing will!'

———

We were suddenly getting an enormous kick out of *The Avengers*. We tried to be offbeat, original. We began to take it seriously... but not too seriously.

The writers would dream up a crisis for us to solve and allow us to bring our own devices to the situation. When Steed needed Cathy's help in one of those wonderfully preposterous situations that are the lifeblood of *The Avengers*, he would gain her interest in an oblique way. He never asked for it directly. He might be polishing a hunting rifle, apparently deep in thought, when she came in. He'd inquire, casually:

"Know anything about the circus?"

"A bit," she replies.

"Good, I've got you a job in the Big Top, as a photographer."

"That sort of thing doesn't appeal to me," she'd answer, impatiently.

Steed would continue polishing the rifle, pretending he didn't care. After a second or two she'd say, "Where's the circus?"

In the next scene she'd be laughing and joking with a circus clown.

The one we did about the circus, 'Conspiracy of Silence', reminds me of an instance when Honor showed courage far beyond the call of duty. To soak up the atmosphere that only the sawdust ring provides, Honor spent some time with the circus people who had set up their equipment in Studio 2 at Teddington several days prior to taping the show. There she did everything from playing a clown (complete with red-nose make-up), to riding around the sawdust ring on horseback, walking on a tightrope (suspended eighteen inches from the ground — the insurance company wouldn't approve anything higher) and, I thought, the bravest thing of all, standing on a rotating turn-table, with her arms and legs pinioned, while a knife-throwing act threw his knives at her as she whirled around and around — apparently without a tremor. I wouldn't have gone near it!

To get this far, Honor and I had forged our way through day after day of energy-sapping rehearsals. Producer Leonard White — and later, John Bryce — would join us during the second week, to make sure that the performances were satisfactory. The director would be there, to instruct the cameramen as to where he wanted to set the cameras. The lighting and sound technicians would put their heads together and discuss any last minute difficulties. The story editor would come onto the set to check that no changes had been made to the script which might affect the narrative.

After ten days' rehearsal, the tempo would increase and the race against the clock hotted up. Fridays were run-through after run-through, and then it was Saturday, the climax of concentrated, grinding work. A dress rehearsal in the afternoon. A short break for a late lunch, and then, in the early evening, the final performance: a vibrant, terrifying time. As the recording nears, tensions reach flashpoint. The heart rate increases. Nerves crack. There is the constant fear that one might dry and forget one's lines. "Come on, loves. Pull your socks up, pull your socks up!" Then, "Stand by VTR!" The videotape recorders roll and, before you knew it, another episode is in the can.

Throughout this time, my respect for Honor

VTR, the final perfor-
mance — a vibrant,
terrifying time.

as an actress and as a person was immense. She had a wonderful sense of integrity and I got very close to her, but I never really talked to Honor about anything deep at all. I shied away from it.

At the time I think she believed that I didn't quite approve of Mrs Gale, and thought that the character was a bit too aggressive and independent. Nothing could have been further from the truth. I *loved* Cathy. I believed in everything Cathy did on screen. I *adored* Honor. She was intelligent, beautiful and quick off the mark.

Steed, of course, continued to reflect the image of sartorial perfection. He cared about wines and pictures, and the graces and beauties of life, which I think at that time was quite important to show.

You see, the strange thing about the English character is that they understate everything. It's considered bad form to comment on the food, money, romance, any of those things. So you underplay it.

If, for instance, anyone said to me, "What's the name of your dog?" and they were referring to an enormous Great Dane, I'd answer,

"Puppy."

They'd stare, quizzically. "Oh, haven't you given him a name then?"

I'd say, "No. He's called Puppy."

A look of astonishment. "But he's so *big*!"

I'd grin and say, "That's why I call him Puppy — he's big, like *Little* John." It's that dichotomy again, the irony of the English character. It was the same with Steed. Whenever anyone asked me why I called the women Mrs or Miss, I'd say, "Well, one always does, doesn't one, until one gets to know them better."

That's very English. At school it was always Macnee, never Patrick, or my middle name, Daniel. Or Major or Minor, as my brother Jimmy was called when he joined us — Macnee Minor. It's part of the English phlegm. If you come from a single sex school, it's extraordinarily difficult to relate to women. I was sending that up... unconsciously and consciously.

Nobody ever knew if Steed and his partners were having an affair, because the English never *look* as though they are having an affair. They may show something by the way that they look at each other, by what they say to each other, by the way that they touch each

other, but not by what they're feeling, ever. So Steed had no feelings. He just reacted.

In those days, Steed and his partner were never employed by anyone. I loved that.

People used to come up and ask me, "Who's your boss?"

I'd say, "Do I have to have one?"

"Well, yes," they'd guffaw. "You're supposed to if you're doing police work."

My reply was to tell them that I was not doing police work. "There's hardly a police-man in the show at all. I do undercover work, well, not even undercover, because I'm obvi-ously so easy to recognise with this bowler hat, umbrella and smart suits."

Midway through the production of Honor's first season, the audience research company TAM published its findings — data that delighted the whole production team:

'Last night Honor Blackman's programme *The Avengers* was seen in an estimated 1,663,000 homes. Miss Millicent Martin was seen in the BBC's *That Was the Week that Was* in about 905,000 homes. Miss Brigitte Bardot, appearing in ITV's *On the Braden Beat*, was seen in an estimated 582,000 homes. Most viewers watched *The Avengers* to the end.'

———

To cut down time travelling to and from the Teddington studios, I had set up home in a modern, unpretentious semi-detached house in Derwent Avenue, at nearby Kingston-upon-Thames.

I'd rise at 6.30am, read the script and set off for the studio, usually around 8.45am. Our working day was from 10am to 9pm. Very often I was the first to arrive on the set. However, my routine was broken in December 1962, when snow fell at Christmas and the temperature dropped to three below. The win-ter of 1962-63 was the coldest in England since 1740. The blizzards and disruption to transport hung around for several weeks and the snow was still a foot deep on New Year's Day. The bitterly cold weather didn't break until early March.

Naturally, this played havoc with the studio schedules, and several actors (including myself) began arriving at the studio's rehearsal room up to ninety minutes late. That we got there at all on some mornings was due to the pertinacity of myself and my trusty Vauxhall. ∎

Clowning about as Father Christmas to Honor's Dick Whitt-ington, while Junia, referred to by me as "Puppy", ponders what goodies lie in store on the Christmas tree.

In 1964, we won the Variety Club of Great Britain award for 1963, which was our golden year.

We received it at the same lunch as The Beatles accepted their award as Joint Personalities of the Year. We were voted Joint Independent Television's Personalities of 1963 and got a medallion to show for it. My name was spelt wrong: Mac, big 'N', double 'e'... I never had it corrected!

I sat next to Billy Butlin and Mike Frankovich, a very famous producer. Butlin said, "Don't take too long will you, boy. By the time I've finished this cigar I'd like to go back to work."

So I didn't. I just thanked Mr Harold Wilson and left the stage.

The awards ceremony was held at the Grosvenor House Hotel. We sat on a raised dais. Harold Wilson was in the centre and we all fanned out on each side of him. The line-up was The Beatles, Wilfred Brambell and Harry H. Corbett (Joint Top BBC Personalities), Jean Metcalfe (BBC Sound Personality), the MC, Harold Wilson, Honor, me, Billy Butlin and Mike Frankovich.

I remember the proud moment when Michael Powell came all the way across the room to greet me. Michael used to be my great idol, the person who employed me when I was little more than an extra. He came up, shook my hand and said, "Congratulations, Pat. It's great. I knew it would happen."

It was our proudest moment in *The Avengers*. After that we never quite achieved anything... well, we *achieved* quite a lot, but we never won another major British award. Nevertheless, we had this award and it was a great feeling. It wasn't the Oscar, but it was the best that television gave in those days.

The producers only gave us about an hour and a half off because the ceremony clashed with rehearsals. I remember that they called us into their office. We sat there like two naughty schoolchildren brought before the headmaster.

"Why're you here?" said an executive. "Ah, yes, this awards thing. Mmm, yes... well, we really can't let you off for very long to attend this thing. Get in there, do it and get back to the set as soon as you can."

We were always coming across instances like that. They liked to put actors down in those days, in case we asked for more money. We

With our awards from the Variety Club. A proud moment, even if my name was spelt wrong!

didn't really realise the power that we had, or the success of the show until that Variety Club award, when everybody who was anybody at ABC attended, because it meant a great deal to the studio.

It's true to say, I think, that *The Avengers* was made in spite of itself. The behaviour of the powerful people who sat in the background was revealing.

At the time I didn't realise this, because I was too busy trying to help make the show good. But I've been able to peruse a few inter-office memos from that time, which show a cynical disregard and contempt for what they

KINKY BOOTS

Caught napping during the dress rehearsal for 'The Grandeur That Was Rome'.

for the casting of each episode. Producer John Bryce and the story editor, Richard Bates, were now limited to, apart from Honor and myself, "X number of 'A' grade actors, Y number of 'B' grade and Z number of 'C' grade, plus extras."

In effect this meant that *The Avengers*, then number one in the ratings, was actually *cutting back* on its spending, when drama shows produced by other ITV companies were increasing their budgets!

That's when Honor and I dropped our own bombshell. Our contracts were up for renewal and we asked for more money!

Alarm bells rang. The balloon went up and the apoplectic board at ABPC threatened us with dismissal... they said one of us had to go! 'We must face up to the fact that we cannot afford Blackman and Macnee,' an executive's memo reveals. 'May a decision please be given, therefore, on the following: Which star is to be dropped? If no star is to be dropped, can approval be given for a £5,100 budget?'

Howard Thomas approved the new budget, despite his colleague having made it patently obvious that he would not like to see my fee increased and suggesting that Honor's be contained at a 'sensible' level! (It's alarming to think that our careers hung on the whim of a man we didn't even know. I'll concede that he was, perhaps, only doing his job — but really!)

In 1964 we were back to a weekly recording pattern. It was just sheer hard work and we felt that we'd worked so hard in this fast-moving, energy-sapping series that the show had taken us over — *The Avengers* was *everything*.

There were happy times, of course. The 'Pat 'n' Honor' (as Peter Hammond used to refer to us, making it sound as though we were one person — Pattern-Honor) time was one.

"Pat 'n' Honor," he'd say, when we returned a few minutes late from the pub. "Pat 'n' Honor, you're late... and Patrick, I suppose you've been drinking?"

"Well, yes. A small glass of wine..." I'd reply.

"Yes. Well, Pat 'n' Honor. You're late."

Peter was always giving me advice about the bowler and umbrella.

I'd say, "Peter. This one takes place down a coal mine. What shall I wear?"

"What else?" he'd answer. "You wear the bowler hat and the umbrella."

"What? Down a coal mine?!"

"Patrick, Steed's his own man *wherever* he is." I never forgot that.

I have fond memories of the time when Honor knocked out wrestler Jackie Pallo — a time so clear in my thoughts because the action (for the episode 'Mandrake') was shot during the week that I celebrated my forty-second birthday.

used to call 'The Talent'.

The ABPC management was forever wailing on about the "spiralling costs of the series", a euphemism for, "We don't want to spend a penny more than we have to on this series," something we'd heard so many times before.

I remember that early in the third season we were told that the ABPC bigwig who looked after the Iris Productions finances (Iris being the subsidiary company set up by ABPC to make the show) had taken "emergency action" to stem the tide of mounting production costs, and had drawn up a new formula

By then we were using five cameras to film Honor's fights. On this occasion Honor and Jackie had to fight in a graveyard set up in the studio. After rehearsing the action, they started the fight in earnest, and one or more of the cameras missed filming the action. Five or six times they did this, each take being aborted because one of the cameramen fluffed the shot. The time came for the last take. Exhausted, Honor dried. Instead of placing her boot on Jackie's face and pushing him backwards into the open grave, as she had done in rehearsal, she lunged for the spade he was carrying. Then, remembering that she was supposed to boot him, she kicked him hard in the face! His nose split and his eyes glazed, but Jackie still remembered his next move, which was to run around the grave and fight Honor for the spade. They fought, she gave him a push and Jackie tumbled backwards into the grave.

The tumble was for real. Jackie was unconscious for six or seven minutes.

Honor told me afterwards that she thought that she'd ruined his career. The incident gave us an extraordinary amount of publicity. Next morning, every newspaper in England carried the story and pictures on its front page.

Leonard White, who had steered the show through fifty or more episodes, had left us midway through the previous season, to pursue a new life. John Bryce now headed up the team as producer, the post of script editor being handed to Richard Bates.

Roger Marshall credits Richard with injecting credibility back into the storylines:

'Richard Bates arrived on the scene. For the first time, someone who mattered thought the visual content should be matched with a script that had a beginning, a middle and an end. Preferably in that order. It was a sea change — the pictures began to talk. Parts became worth acting, so worth offering to decent actors. People like Andre Morrell, Philip Madoc, Philip Locke, John Le Mesurier, John Laurie and Warren Mitchell came to pit their wits against our dynamic duo... and to lose. A very young John Thaw made his initial appearance at Teddington, to return a couple of years later with his first starring role (in *Redcap*). For the first time, stories were being told on screen with wit and style. Yes, the set did shudder

'When the taped series was at its considerable peak, it was recommended for a Writers' Guild award. Eric Paice, who should've known better, rejected it on the grounds that it was a director's piece, *not* a writer's. That had been true once, but it wasn't any more.'

A canny Scot, John Bryce was very sensitive to criticism, particularly when confronted with the comment that *The Avengers* was conceived as a satire of counter-espionage thrillers, but the viewers insisted on taking it *seriously*!

Livid when people insisted on calling the show a 'formula' series, he went out of his way to make the series more adventurous, more tongue-in-cheek — better.

At one point, we even discussed a story in which Cathy would be tied to the railway tracks, *à la* Pearl White. The idea was abandoned (at least until Diana Rigg joined us) as being almost impossible to achieve — to fake — in the studio.

The fights — which weren't really very good in the previous series, but worked because of the style and strength of the scripts — were now being filmed on the day before the 'live' recording, giving an edge to Honor's athleticism not seen in the second season shows.

By now Honor had achieved a brown belt at judo and was seen as a kind of role model by women, who realised that they *could* defend themselves from muggers. This was before the problem was widely recognised as existing, of course (and long before the advent of Mace).

By now, as **Sydney Newman** recalls, ABC TV was inundated with sacks of mail addressed to 'Cathy Gale' and 'John Steed':

'The weekly fan mail sent to Pat and Honor increased to drowning levels. The diversity of people was truly awe inspiring. Leonard and I were too innocent of the ways of the world to anticipate that we would be catering to the few kinky, S & M nuts inevitable in any mass audience, because of Honor's clothes. One day Honor came to me and showed me a letter which upset her greatly.

'I read: 'On a foggy night as I think of you I can't wait to take all my clothes off, put on my rubber mac and go out into the foggy night walking with the slithery rubber sliding across my bare skin...' The sex of the writer was unknown because it was unsigned. Ugh, I thought, what the hell had we wrought? Honor begged to be relieved of having to answer the bulk of the letters. Marie Donaldson, our inspired PR head, took on the chore of looking after fan mail.'

occasionally and the door stuck at the wrong moment. But who cared? Friendships made then survive thirty years later.

'At the time no television show achieved such enormous popularity and critical esteem. Everyone was talking *Avengers*. It became part of 'Swinging London', along with the King's Road, Carnaby Street, Twiggy, George Best, Mary Quant and other such icons.

'The show was enormous fun to work on. I'm sure there were tantrums and hair-tearing, but it's hard to recall them. At one recording I sensed an atmosphere and was told that, "Pat's verruca's playing up." On another occasion I was temporarily in the dog-house: "Honor's got more lines in part two!" Not exactly grounds for divorce!

In 1964, Honor and I, who had done some unlikely things in our time, were invited to make a record!

At first I refused. Tone-deaf, the thought of entering a recording studio was the furthest thing from my mind.

After much persuasion, we recorded two numbers, 'Kinky Boots' and 'Keep It Friendly', both written by Herbert Kretzmer and Benny Lee, who had also written the Peter Sellers/ Sophia Loren hits. (Herbie Kretzmer would eventually write the English lyrics for the award-winning musical, *Les Misérables*.)

I remember that the recording took place on a Saturday night, after a hard day's rehearsal on *The Avengers*. The problem was, try as I might, I couldn't follow the tune or sing the lyrics when I was supposed to! Honor, who had never set foot in a recording studio before, wasn't in the least bit fazed. After several abortive attempts, she and the record producer escorted me to the local pub. Dutch courage was induced by several brandies — Honor, sensibly, drank lemonade — and we returned to the studio. The sound engineer cued the music, Honor sang and I dried! Faced with disaster, the producer delegated a sound engineer to stand by my side and tap me on the shoulder whenever I was supposed to sing. Several hours later, the record was in the can.

The producer told the press afterwards, "Honor sounds like a cross between Julie London and Marlene Dietrich, and Patrick Macnee has a humorous British twinkle in his timbre." (Patrick Macnee was *terrified*!)

The record was released... and it bombed!

Then, when I thought it had been long forgotten, the single was reissued in 1990 and entered the hit parade, reaching number three in the charts. At one stage, advance sales were in excess of 40,000 copies!

'An inspired reissue for this magnificent high-camp curiosity,' wrote one critic. 'A good novelty song — and a bit naughty into the bargain,' thought another. Not surprising, with lyrics like: 'Fashion magazines say wear 'em and you will all rush to obey like the women in a harem. Sweet girls, street girls, frumpy little beat girls. Square girls, cool girls, sexy little schoolgirls wear 'em!...'

Stories had been circulating around the studio for some time that a 'big American producer' wanted to make a film whose ancestry could be traced legitimately to *The Avengers*.

Encouraged by this — I rather fancied the idea, as did Honor — I spoke to Howard Thomas, who arranged for me to meet a man called Louis de Rochemont.

We met at The Carlton Towers, in Knightsbridge. De Rochemont listened to what I had to say, before presenting me with his own concept of the proposed film's storyline. (It wasn't

until sometime later that I discovered the summary he'd presented to me as his own had in fact been written by Brian Clemens.) I came away from the meeting with the feeling that Steed and Cathy would soon be winging their way to a (profitable) career on the big screen.

Everyone at ABPC gave the project their full support. Programme controller Brian Tesler thought the idea was a natural and that the present production unit was best suited to make it. John Bryce believed the team knew *The Avengers'* style so well, and its appeal so explicitly, that the film could be made easily and swiftly. Howard Thomas gave the project his blessing.

Nothing happened! The film never got made! In the blink of an eye the de Rochemont

Top: Recording 'Kinky Boots'.

Above: Honor looks apprehensive at the prospect of appearing on Thank Your Lucky Stars, *to promote 'Kinky Boots'. (Also pictured, DJ Brian Matthew.)*

film was seen as *the* most attractive proposition. At the drop of a hat it was forgotten! To this day I have no idea exactly why. So we were left with the television series and our Variety Club award, but even that was sullied when I fell out with Honor.

It happened at the end of production party in 1964. Honor and I had done an awful lot of preparation for it and the party was a huge success. During the evening, Honor came up to me and said, "Pat, you didn't invite security!"

This shook me. I'd invited just about everybody else but hadn't thought of the security people.

"Well, it's too late now," continued Honor, "they're manning the main gate. Perhaps we can arrange a drink for them afterwards?" She said this without rancour, but I took it badly. I screamed at her and told her to go to Hell!

Hurt and confused, she turned away with tears in her eyes.

I'd been drinking, of course. When I drank scotch I was a different person. (As Diana Rigg said to me once, when I was due to meet Her Royal Highness Princess Margaret, "Please don't drink scotch, will you, Pat." I asked her why

not? She replied, "Because, Pat... just *because*...")

This happened during the very week we attended the awards ceremony together. Indeed, as I learned later, it was almost to the day when Honor had told ABPC that she wouldn't be staying with the show! I didn't know anything about this at the time. They must have known — she must have told them — but *they* never told me!

When I found out, I was devastated. I simply couldn't believe it... I didn't *want* to believe it. We'd been given this great bonus by the Variety Club — and Honor was leaving!

I remember someone once saying that the two of us didn't seem to have any envy of each other. "You don't appear to have any highs and lows. You just seem to be two happy, comfortable people." And we were.

At the time, it struck me that perhaps it had been agreed everyone at the studio should be told but me. But I distinctly remember that Howard Thomas looked stunned when Honor told him she was leaving during a meeting she had with the ABPC executives on board the *MV Iris*, the boat the company had moored at Teddington Dock, so perhaps they didn't have any inkling that she was actually leaving.

A few weeks later, I was back on board the *MV Iris* again.

"Here you are, Pat."

Beaming like a Cheshire cat, Howard Thomas handed me a card. Typewritten, it said, 'To Patrick Macnee, part owner of *The Avengers!*'

Bemused by his generosity I asked, "But what does this mean?"

"You're staying with us, Pat," he said, explaining that I would have to wait until the show returned, this time made on film, to reap the rewards.

How long would that take?

"It could take months," he said. "We've got some different people coming in. They're doing it at Elstree, Borehamwood. They've just finished a medical series with Herbert Lom, called *The Human Jungle*. You'll be working with Julian Wintle. It's going to be wonderful, Pat!"

I didn't feel wonderful. I felt desolated and wondered if we would ever get to make this new series.

Apprehensive of what the future might hold for *The Avengers*, I returned to my home and addressed my concerns to Howard Thomas:

April 10
Dear Howard,

Thank you so much for your lovely present. I was very touched.

I have just finished working for ATV in one of their *Love Story* episodes. I enjoyed it enormously, wearing a pair of horn-rimmed spectacles and a forward haircut, like Peter Sellers. It is shown on May 19th.

It would be very nice if you and I could meet in the near future. Obviously, ever since you broached the idea to me of some sort of participation in the future of *The Avengers*, my mind has been very active in ideas. I don't know how far you have progressed over the filmed series idea, but to be able to be in at the early stages of artistic planning, as an associate producer, would obviously be very stimulating to me.

To take a very simple premise, of an example of where I feel we could so easily fall into a trap, is the replacement of Honor Blackman. People seem to forget that, marvellous as Honor was, she could not have succeeded had not the idea of her character been such an original one. We should not, in my opinion, *just* replace Honor, but devise another character of equal, but quite different, interest.

Also, the character of Steed needs developing and strengthening, not just updating. All this I am sure you have considered. But my interest in *The Avengers* is so close, that I would like to express myself in the *vital* early, planning stages.

My letter to Howard Thomas.

I imagine it will be very difficult to speed up the antiquated lighting and limited visual activities of Elstree, but unless we can, I feel we will have a constipated series. We can really learn from Hollywood, despite the union difficulties, on matters of technical speed. I dread the thought that *The Avengers* will first go onto film and lose its own identity. Because its whole strength was its elusive appeal. I always quote *The Avengers* as an example of successful transference of a body of live TV talents to film. Also there is no need for an episode to take two weeks. It can easily be done in eight days maximum.

It would, to me, be a triumph if we could be the first English TV series (apart from *Robin Hood*) that got a decent sale in the US. And it could so easily happen.

I like Louis de Rochemont very much, but have a deep fear that he will never get off the ground with the film. It is only a 'hunch', but a strong one.

I enclose a letter from a gentleman who (apart from Honor's series in The *Mail*) has got a remarkable talent for good ideas. I think this is one. The more ways we can make *The*

THE AVENGERS 2 AGAINST THE UNDERWORLD IN THIS EXCITING SERIES OF HOUR LONG PROGRAMMES FOR TELEVISION

A promotional brochure for the Honor Blackman series.

Avengers part of cops-and-robbers folklore the better, don't you agree?

Anyway, it would be wonderful to chat. I am a little concerned, as I am getting various offers, which I am not anxious to accept, as I feel they will deflect me from the main purpose of making *The Avengers* bigger and better.

Yours,
Pat

I never heard a word from Howard Thomas, or anyone else at ABPC for that matter!

I discovered later that they had mounted a silent campaign to deny me access to Julian Wintle and the whole film process. The memos brought this vividly into focus. That Howard Thomas had dared to offer me a post as producer was, according to one executive, tantamount to opening 'the floodgates of discord.'

Concerned that ABPC might get involved in direct conversations with me without Julian Wintle or himself being aware of the situation, but appreciating that they would have to speak to my agent sometime, the executive cautioned: 'I do hope we are not going to be too much involved with *direct* conversations

with Pat Macnee, without Julian Wintle or myself being aware of the situation. We could be placed in an embarrassing position if suggestions have been made to Macnee of which we are not aware.'

And, a few days later, he cited: 'Following the conclusion of the new BFPA Agreement, you instructed me to speak with Julian Wintle about its effects on *The Avengers* series and Pat Macnee's contract. I again spoke to Julian Wintle and stated to him — and this was certainly *prior* to the conclusion of any contract made with Macnee — that any negotiations should *exclude* the question of any percentages of profits arising out of the sales of the series. Julian Wintle accepted this advice.'

What alarmed me most when reading this were two sections of a paragraph that expressed a totally contradictory view of the facts as I understood them:

'It is understood by Macnee that he will not now be designated associate producer and will in fact have no formal production title or role whatsoever. He will, however, be invited to contribute to the planning sessions on the new series, particularly where his own character is concerned, since he feels that he may have several useful suggestions to make with regard to characterisation, stories and style,' and, 'Macnee will be offered a small participation in the profits of the series, the size of which it will be up to you to negotiate in your customary manner.'

What the hell was this man talking about? No one had said anything to me about the possibility of my getting involved in the new series as a producer. I hadn't broached this with anyone. I hadn't even *considered* it... well, perhaps I had, but I knew that such a request would be futile. As for negotiating a percentage of the profits, my understanding was that I was a shareholder already, as acknowledged by the card from Howard Thomas.

No I wasn't! The card (which, in my innocence, I valued so highly) was apparently without value or merit. I was indeed obliged to negotiate the terms of my new contract.

As **Richard Hatton**, who was my agent at the time, recalls, the negotiations were conducted in a manner ill-befitting gentlemen:

'I remember that Pat was one of the few actors who had an understanding of the factors to be considered from a production point of view and the immense amount of consideration that Pat put into casting. I can also remember an absolutely ghastly meeting I had with somebody who was highly placed at the time in an attempt to get them to pay more money than Pat was contracted for, only to be told that privately and on the side they had lent him a large sum of money and I was an ungrateful so-and-so for even daring to raise the question.'

Can you believe it!? I'd done three seasons of *The Avengers*, seventy-eight shows in all, and still they were saying, "Not a penny more!"

Two days later, I was called in to Julian Wintle's office.

He said, "Patrick, dear boy. You really can't ask for *five* per cent of the profits! I mean, I'm sorry, but if you want that you'll have to go. We don't need you. We'll get somebody else... a younger man!"

I was petrified. I had two children growing up, I'd lived a pretty ropey life anyway, and I certainly didn't have much in my savings account.

"A... Al... All right," I stammered. "What *can* I have?"

"Two and a half per cent!" he said in a matter of fact way.

I nodded. That would do.

The ABPC executive had the final word on the subject: 'Thank you for your memo of the 11th concerning Pat Macnee's participation share of the profits of this series,' he wrote to Julian Wintle. 'I think we have all learned some lessons from this transaction.'

Today, that tiny two and a half per cent is, to me, like gold. It was entirely due to Richard Hatton that I got it.

That was one of the many intangibles during that period. There were others. What, for instance, might have happened if Honor had stayed and not done Pussy Galore? Would *The Avengers* still have become one of Britain's most successful television shows throughout the world?

Yes, because Honor was an exceptional person. When she came to us she was already deeply experienced in film and would have easily adapted her performance in the same way that I did when Julian Wintle took over the production.

If Honor and I had taken the show forwards, if we had been more caring, closer to the employers — instead of being manipulated by them — we might have said to each other, "We're into something good, something big, let's make it better." We would have made four seasons together, maybe five.

A filmed series with Honor would have been *so* good. It would have become enormously successful. It would have become the biggest import to the United States you could possibly imagine. Not only that, but we would have started it right away. As it was, we had to wait to get another woman, another production team, and film tests with an actress who essentially didn't work out, then more tests with more actresses.

Lobster Quadrille

All good things come to an end, but that doesn't make the parting easier. Whereas Steed and Doctor Keel never actually ended their partnership on screen, thereafter the producers always found a novel way of changing Steed's partners in mid-stream. The die was cast when Honor left to join 007.

'Lobster Quadrille' (Episode #78, by Richard Lucas, this scene scripted by Brian Clemens).

Scene 28 (271) INT. STUDIO. STEED'S FLAT. DAY.
CATHY IS DRINKING TEA.
STEED: You really look wonderful, my dear.
STEED TAKES EMPTY CUP. PLACES IT ON BUREAU.
CATHY: Thank you.
STEED: And I've hung you in a place of honour.
POINTS TO PORTRAIT OF CATHY POSITIONED ABOVE BUREAU.
CATHY: Yes. Very touching.
STEED: I told you a couple of days' complete relaxation would work wonders. How are the burns by the way?
CATHY: Only superficial.
STEED: Good. I'm delighted to hear it, cause... (HE CROSSES ROOM. OPENS CABINET. REMOVES BOX, HANDS IT TO CATHY.) I've got something for you. To replace the wardrobe you lost in the — er — line of fire.
CATHY: Ah, that's nice. (SHE OPENS BOX, REMOVES PACKING, TAKES OUT ONE-PIECE BATHING SUIT.) Who told you?
STEED (JOCULAR): Told me what?
CATHY: That I'm taking a holiday.
STEED: *Are you*!?
CATHY: Yes. I leave tomorrow.

I'm off to the Bahamas.
STEED SITS. SMILES.
STEED: *No*! What an extraordinary coincidence... As a matter of fact there's just a...
FAVOUR CATHY.
CATHY: A tiny bit of trouble out there?
STAY WITH CATHY.
STEED: That's right! Nothing dangerous, of course.
CATHY (CYNICAL): No, no. Of course not.
FAVOUR STEED.
STEED (BRIGHT): As you're going to be out there anyway, pussy-footing along those sun-soaked shores...
WITH CATHY.
CATHY: I might as well do a little investigating?
STEED: That's the idea. What do you say?
CATHY: *Goodbye*, Steed!
STEED: Eh?
CATHY REPLACES COSTUME IN BOX. RISES.
CATHY: That's what I say. *Goodbye*.
STEED: Oh, but that isn't asking too much...
FAVOUR CATHY.
CATHY (DETERMINED): *Yes* it is! You see, I shan't be pussy-footing along those sun-soaked beaches, I'll be *lying* on them.
CATHY EXITS.
STEED: No *pussy-footing*? I must have been misinformed.
HE PICKS UP TELEPHONE, RECLINES ON COUCH, DIALS NUMBER, SPEAKS TO SOMEONE. (O.C.)

FADE TO BLACK GRAMS (24)
F/U Theme

And with that sly reference to her character in the film, Honor was off to make *Goldfinger*. ■

'Build a Better Mousetrap'.

So I never had a chance to make a filmed series with Honor. What eventually happened *was* tremendously successful, but it was not what I would have liked, at least not then.

I knew all along, of course, that Honor wasn't deserting us. However, the fact that she left when she did was nevertheless a lasting source of sorrow. Many years later, I met Cubby Broccoli and asked him, in a light-hearted way, why had he taken Honor Blackman away from us? "But, Patrick," he said, "she could have done both!" She might well have done so, but the two of us knew that it wasn't to be. When she joined us, her original contract was for six shows, with options. After about six months or so, her contract came up for renewal and they wanted her to sign for another two years. She told them no. "I'll do it for two years in all, not a day longer. When my contract expires I'm gone." This coincided with the offer from Cubby Broccoli to appear in

Goldfinger. So it was right that she moved on to pastures anew and flirted in the hay with 007. Indeed, the one Bond heroine who had the strength of character to mix it with Bond was Pussy Galore. Honor was like that.

And what of the producers? Around that time, Richard Bates and John Bryce came around to see me in my apartment.

"Pat," they said. "Why can't *we* do the filmed series? Will you please put in a good word for us with Julian Wintle, because we would like to do the same job, which we've done so successfully with the taped series."

I didn't... well, maybe I did say something, but I certainly didn't fight in their corner as well as I might have done, as I *should* have done. That I didn't was probably one of the most cowardly actions of my professional life.

I should have pushed harder for these two men who had orchestrated for Honor and myself the Variety Club award, and had made the two of us synonymous with success. That they came to *me*, to ask me to represent their case, and I didn't, is a terrible indictment.

Then again, as **Roger Marshall** recalls events, perhaps my request would have fallen on deaf ears:

'Pat Macnee, all Old Etonian charm and elegance, allied with Honor in this strange 'do they, don't they?' partnership, had taken the television thriller into an entirely new direction. There was no blueprint, no template, it just evolved. By now everyone was pressing hard for the series to go on film. The company stalled, the James Bond offer came and Honor left.

'In command of the cameras was a nucleus of like-minded, stylish young directors: Peter Hammond, Don Leaver, Bill Bain and Kim Mills. Richard Bates was hiring writers he knew could deliver. Because he trusted them, he allowed them to write what they wanted to write rather than what he told them to. Sad to relate, it wouldn't quite be like that ever again. Not I suggest for deliberate reasons. Rather that there were too few people trying to do too many jobs. Peter Hammond, famous for his mirror shots, did more than anyone to establish the *Avengers* look. Neither he nor Kim Mills ever worked at Elstree. Don and Bill did so, but only sporadically. Their alleged 'crime' was that they didn't know film. Despite the great episodes that were still to come, this decision was — for my money — the most significant error of judgement made by the Wintle/Fennell regime.'

I didn't know it at the time, but we wouldn't actually start shooting *The Avengers* on film until nine months after the taped series ended!

On location with Ian Carmichael at Maer Hall in Staffordshire, during location filming for ABC TV's presentation of The Importance of Being Earnest.

I didn't work in television again until November 1964, when ABC TV invited me to play Algie Moncrieff to Ian Carmichael's Jack Worthing, in their *Armchair Theatre* presentation of Oscar Wilde's witty, elegant and absurdly funny *The Importance of Being Earnest*.

Sharing the honours with Ian and myself were Susannah York, Fenella Fielding, Irene Handl, Pamela Brown and Wilfred Brambell.

A supreme actress, Irene Handl was a dear, sweet woman. Throughout the rehearsal, she had her pet Chihuahua with her. If you came too close to her, it would reach out and bite you. At the time, Irene was perpetually writing a massive 'family saga' novel called *The Sioux*. She would clutch the book tightly to her bosom and write in it at every available opportunity. She eventually published it to enormous success.

Hearing that I wasn't good on the lines, Ian used to pick me up in his car from my apartment, and we'd go through the dialogue con-

stantly as we drove to the studio in Teddington, then do it all again in the rehearsal rooms. This routine continued right up until the day of recording.

We started the show, and performed it so fast that after about twenty minutes, Bill Bain, the director, said, "We have to stop!" We thought there had been a train accident, or an explosion or something, because you *never* stopped.

He said, "I just have to tell you — you're both so nervous, you're going so fast, that we can't hear anything."

Being extra long, the TV network had scheduled the play for a transmission slot of seventy-five minutes. At the speed we were performing it, if Bill hadn't stopped us, Wilde's classic would have been over and done with in sixty minutes flat!

I've seen it recently and it's lovely, but that first act is still very, very fast. ■

smile now when I remember Howard Thomas saying to me, "Stay close to Julian Wintle and his team, Pat. They know about film. Just go in there and find out what their thinking is."

I couldn't seem to get locked into the idea of going over to film. I really thought that I'd had enough. Honor and I had been an unbeatable pairing, one that could never be replaced.

Then I went out to lunch with Brian Clemens, who had always seemed to me the most structured and ordered of people. So when he told me to stop worrying, I listened. I thought to myself, if *he* is going to be part of the new team, it really will work, because he has the knowledge and expertise required to turn things around and make it a success.

"You really shouldn't spend your time worrying about the show, Pat," he told me. "When it folds up in one area, it will start up in another. You're always too anxious."

I suppose I was. But I was in the middle of something that promised to be wonderful. I was working in this extraordinary show and I was only halfway through it. I realised then that I didn't want it to end.

———

So it came close to the time when we were to commence filming. The excitement of starting again was increased by this strange sort of new beginning. By now I'd moved from Kingston-upon-Thames and had rented a flat in Swiss Cottage, just a comfortable drive from the studio at Elstree. It was there that I met ABC Television's choice as the successor to Honor Blackman, an extraordinarily beautiful woman called Beth Shepherd. Similar to Honor Blackman in many ways, she arrived with her long hair brushed to one side and tied up in a long bob. (Combed out, it was light and wispy and shone like threads of golden gossamer). Slim, her figure was better proportioned than Honor's, but I couldn't help thinking that Honor's bone structure, when suitably emphasised, created a more sexy effect than Beth's more rounded contours.

She arrived in clothes by Bonnie Cashin, a

HOW TO SUCCEED... IN AMERICA

*Elizabeth Shepherd,
ABC TV's first choice
for Emma Peel.*

famous designer of the time, who shopped out of Debenham and Freebody, or Saks Fifth Avenue. All frightfully swingy and suave, she indicated to Julian Wintle that this was the kind of wardrobe she believed she should wear for the series, because the look suited her personality.

Unimpressed, Albert Fennell arranged camera tests to check the suitability of her wardrobe and make-up. His concern was judicious, as the majority of the Bonnie Cashin outfits were not suitable. Everything that made them beautiful and dramatic in reality was lost or distorted on screen. He decided that Beth Shepherd would require a brand new wardrobe, one that was theatrically effective, dramatic and strikingly unusual.

There was no time to organise this; filming of the first show was scheduled to begin in forty-eight hours. The decision was taken to shoot using the most alluring outfits in her wardrobe, which had already cost £500!

Harry Pottle joined the production team as art director (production designer in today's parlance) on a cold, mid-November day in 1964, when they were preparing the series:

'When the series was in the prep stage, director Peter Graham Scott thought it would be a good idea if Beth Shepherd told me how she thought Emma Peel's apartment should look. I met her in her dressing room. Her ideas reflected her personal taste and not the one that was visualised for the character. Albert Fennell was also expressing his concern at the amount of money that had been spent on Beth's wardrobe. He resolved the problem in his usual quiet, but efficacious manner.'

Peter Graham Scott had been hired to direct the first episode:

'When Julian Wintle asked me to come and do the first episode (what was *scheduled* to be the first episode, it didn't turn out that way), I was a bit iffy about taking it on. I read the script for this thing called 'The Town of No Return' and told Julian, "I really don't know about this. This thing has got to have *very* distinctive direction. It calls for odd angles, and we've got to keep it punching along — every ten minutes or so we've got to come up with a big climax." The script had a strange, indefinable something where, suddenly in the course of the action, you come around the corner and there's something very bizarre. Julian agreed, that was the way he saw things too.

'I knew that Beth Shepherd had been cast and I was looking forward to working with her again. She had worked for me before on television. She'd been in a thing called *The Citadel* and she was very, very good. But, of course, that was her sort of part — classy, a bit glacial. She'd also done a programme called *Doctor Everyman's Hour*, in which she was tremendous. She was a very powerful actress, there's no doubt about that.

'We started filming and I remember that we did this tracking shot in a pub. It had been set up with props from World War Two. Patrick was supposed to walk by these things and try them on while he's talking to the girl, then she'd play around with them — it was a good plot device. We did it and it worked very well. Then we went on location to Hunstanton, in Norfolk.

'We filmed the scenes at the airport, with Patrick and Beth wandering around, and I thought that Beth Shepherd was getting a bit of fun out of it. Then, curiously, when we saw the rushes, the scenes with Beth Shepherd hadn't got any fire in them. They lacked passion — that hidden fire that I knew she had, that sort of 'hidden-under-glass' sex appeal somehow wasn't coming off the screen. And the humour, the twinkle in the eye, wasn't there.

'After several days' filming in Norfolk, Beth joined me for dinner one night and said, "I think the key to this woman is her watch."

'"Her *what?*" I asked.

'"Her watch... It's got a chronometer."

'"Um, and...??" I said.

'Beth continued, "If she has this chronometer on it which tells her everything, then I don't need ever to appear to have to read up on everything. I just press this chronometer, look at it and say, 'Ah, the answer is...'"

'Politely, I pointed out that this wasn't very visual.

'"Isn't it?" she enquired.

'I shook my head. That's when I first thought that maybe she didn't understand what punchy television was all about.'

I wouldn't argue with that (but that chronometer idea, in retrospect, was interesting). She really had very little understanding of this strange character, this woman who was — had been — Cathy Gale, a woman of decision and energy. Unfortunately, Beth Shepherd was one of those women who when she ran, flapped her arms — as most women do, and that's fine and attractive and sweet. However, for a hermaphrodite part like Cathy Gale (or in this case, Emma Peel), where you really needed to look like a boy scout if only from the waist downwards, it wasn't right. The girl needed to be fleet and fast and determined. Beth wasn't.

We tried everything to overcome this, but to no avail. Beautiful, she looked just wonderful in close-ups. She was very fond and very dear, yet somehow I knew that it wasn't going to work. Beth Shepherd as Emma Peel was a

square peg in a round hole. She never really got the point of *The Avengers*, but neither did I at that time. *I* hadn't got a pointer on Steed — on *how* the new producers wanted me to play Steed. I wanted them to study what Honor and I had done, to see if they were going to replicate something that I thought was pretty perfect. I had strong reservations that they would not be able to, so I begged them to watch the earlier shows. Now, when I look back on the Honor Blackman episodes, as good as Honor was, they serve as a reminder that we had to do them off the cuff, which wasn't easy at all.

We filmed the whole of this episode, a strange story which had a very exciting element to it, with people living in a village taking on the identities of other people who had all been killed. By this time I was wishing that someone would take over the identity of John Steed, or at least replace the woman by his side.

Then, strangely enough, one day when I was

With Elizabeth Shepherd during the filming of 'The Town of No Return'. The show was later remade with Diana Rigg. (Picture courtesy of Brian Clemens.)

A publicity card for Diana's first season.

A
Series of
26 ONE HOUR
PROGRAMMES
for TELEVISION

WATCH OUT FOR THE AVENGERS

starring:
PATRICK MACNEE as JOHN STEED
DIANA RIGG as EMMA PEEL

filming a scene for the second story, 'The Murder Market', with Patrick Cargill and a few others in a graveyard near Fulham, they came and told us that Beth Shepherd had been fired. They'd paid her off and she'd gone. Patrick Cargill looked into the open grave, beside which he and I were standing, turned to me and said, "Alas, poor Beth. I never even *met* her, y'know."

So what did we do? We did tests.

Filmed over several days, the auditions were directed by **Peter Graham Scott**:

'We finished the film with Beth Shepherd,

put it together and Howard Thomas saw it in the preview theatre. There was a terrible silence at the end of it. Nobody spoke. Then Howard said, "We've got to fire this girl!"

'And that was it — we stopped production. "Come in tomorrow," said Howard. "Plot three typical *Avengers* scenes. We'll have a lot of girls lined up and we'll do tests." So that's what we did.

'There were some very good girls there, one of whom, I remember, was Shirley Eaton. She was a very pretty girl with a great sense of humour. She, I thought, was a strong candidate, as was Moira Redmond, whom I felt was

a little too old for the part.

'One of the girls I'd met about a year earlier, at Julian's home, curiously enough, during a New Year's party. It was one of those things where it was very crowded and someone knocked a plate of sandwiches from my hand. As I bent down to pick them up, I noticed a young girl lying under the piano and this wonderful voice said, "Hello. Who are you?" It was Diana Rigg.

'For some reason or other, shooting the tests took ages. Time was running away from us when I'd finished filming the other girls, and we still hadn't got round to Diana. I knew that we didn't have time to do another set-up, so I said to the cameraman, "We'll do a wonderful portrait in close-up. We'll let her read the lines and we'll see how she does with it." That was the sum total of Diana's test.

'At the end of the day I went over to Diana and said, "I'm very sorry. You realise that we were pushed for time, but I really think I've lost you this job." She said, "Well, Peter, I didn't really want it anyway." She didn't appear to be

Above: With stunt arranger Ray Austin on the seashore at St Mary's Bay in Kent.

Left: Ray Austin and Diana during a photo publicity shoot at St Mary's Bay.

Above: Diana throwing Ray Austin (left) and stuntman Billy Cornelius (right) across the studio.

Right: Ray puts Diana through her paces.

bothered. She knew that she could always go back to the RSC.

'So that was it. Somewhere near to the end of the tests came a close-up of this girl with the lovely whispering voice and wonderful eyes. The rest, as they say, is history.'

By this time I was about to get married to my girlfriend Kate. When I told her that Beth Shepherd had gone she said, naturally enough, "Well, *I've* got to test." And she did. A lot of actresses did. And Diana Rigg won, without question, although I didn't even see her test. Wintle, Fennell, Clemens and Howard Thomas chose her. I actually met Diana after they'd tested her. We did a vignette together for the camera.

I met Ray Austin for the first time on the filmed series. A stunt arranger *par excellence*, he was wonderful to be with. He still is.

An extraordinarily forthright man, he'd had many interesting jobs, including a time as Cary Grant's chauffeur, and had a tremendous background in stunting for television and film. Ray also had a very varied background in all sorts of other ways. He'd studied camera

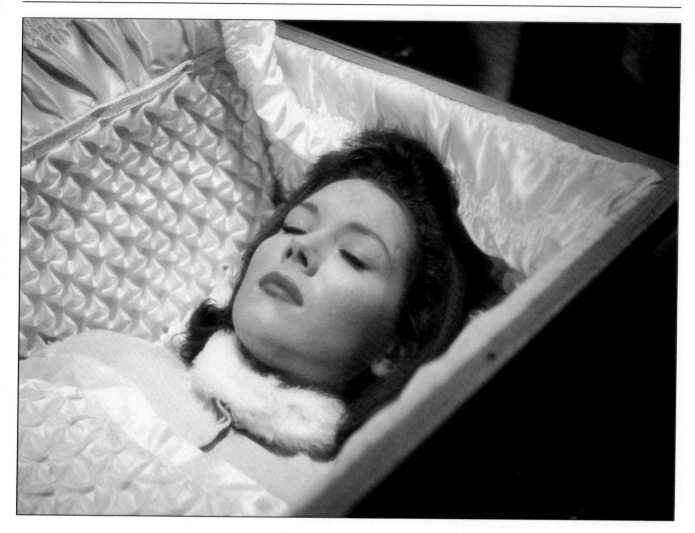

technique and had ambitions of becoming a director, which he did, his early work including several episodes of *The New Avengers*. From that he leapt into Hollywood and has worked solidly as a director ever since.

Devising fights is directly related to what you can do on film. Ray was able to bring something to the show that was almost impossible to achieve with any degree of realism in the taped series; gutsy, fast-moving action, particularly with the balletic mode of fighting he created for Emma Peel.

Ray Austin was handed the pleasurable task of getting to grips with the women on the judo mat:

'As well as testing a dialogue scene with Pat, Diana, like all the other candidates, had to do a fight scene with me. After a week of this with different actresses, I was black and blue, because of their enthusiasm. Enter Diana.

'Tall, good figure, legs that seemed to go on forever (*that's* why the fights looked so good, not my orchestrating), she was reliable in her fight test. Meaning, if I told her to hit me with a right, she did not surprise me and land a left

from out of the blue and kick me in the balls for good measure. The bosses looked at her test — she became Emma Peel.'

So Diana was kitted out, and given some lessons by Ray on how to tumble and fall. Not that she needed it, as she could move beautifully already. She had a gorgeous, direct carriage, a wonderful voice, stunning auburn hair and a look of flashing insolence.

I thought, "My God. I've got to get to know her!" So I took her to dinner at the Connaught Hotel.

We were both perfectly outrageous, obviously trying to test each other's limits of what we liked and didn't like, and naturally everything gravitated to sex. Di said she only made exceptions for men of intellect, and gave me a withering look which suggested that I didn't fit the bill. I realised then that we had this strange communion.

The very next day we went to work!

———

I remember that we had a scene in my apartment (for the episode 'The Murder Market') and I was supposed to play the tuba, because I

Mrs Peel — 'dead'. It's a ruse, of course, this time to allow Steed to tear apart the machinations of the Togetherness Marriage Bureau. (From 'The Murder Market'.)

The Town of No Return

Written by Brian Clemens, this was filmed as the pilot (with Beth Shepherd as Mrs Peel), then refilmed as episode #93) with Diana Rigg.

Beautifully crafted, the introductory scenes between Mrs Peel and Steed are a joy — and very funny.

The Town of No Return' (Episode # , by Brian Clemens).

EXT. EMMA PEEL'S APARTMENT. DAY.
STEED: Good morning, Mrs Peel.
EMMA: Good morning, Steed. The door's open.

INT. EMMA PEEL'S APARTMENT. DAY.
STEED ENTERS. EMMA, ATTIRED IN FENCING GARB, IS PRACTISING ÉPÉE ROUTINE. TURNING, SHE CROSSES SWORDS WITH STEED'S UMBRELLA.
EMMA: Social visit?
THE TIP OF HER ÉPÉE SNAKES OUT TO LIE AT THE BASE OF STEED'S NECK.
STEED: That's it. Happened to be passing by — thought I'd drop in.
EMMA REMOVES FACE GUARD. STEED DOFFS BOWLER. SHE MOTIONS TO A TABLE.
EMMA: The coffee's over there.
SHE MOVES ASIDE. STEED REACHES TABLE, TURNS. EMMA CONTINUES PRACTICE MOVEMENTS.
STEED: Not enough flexibility in the wrist... (SHE IGNORES THIS.) Weight on the wrong foot... (SHE TURNS. HER SWORD FINDS STEED'S RIBS. STEED'S ARMS RAISED) *Friendly* advice...
EMMA REMOVES ÉPÉE.
STEED (BEAT): There doesn't appear to be any *cream*.
EMMA INDICATES KITCHEN WITH SWORD.
EMMA: The *cream*... is in the kitchen.
HE MOVES TOWARDS DOOR. EMMA HAS HIM AT SWORDPOINT AGAIN.
STEED: I could take it *black*.
EMMA ARMS HIM WITH AN ÉPÉE. STANDS EN GARDE. STEED PICKS UP

A FACE MASK. THEY DON MASKS, SALUTE EACH OTHER, ENGAGE IN FRIENDLY COMBAT.
STEED: By the way... are you busy just now?
EMMA: Not very. I've just written an article for *Science Weekly* — but that's finished... (HE LEAP-FROGS CHAIR. SHE SMACKS HIM ON REAR.) Why?
STEED: Oh, just interested. Marvellous day today... certainly not the sort of day to be stuck in town, is it?
DRIVEN BACKWARDS, HE TUMBLES INTO CHAIR.
STEED (PANTS): We ought to get away... down to the coast for a while.
EMMA (IN CONTROL):*We?*
SHE TURNS, WALKS AWAY. A MISTAKE. STEED TAPS HER GENTLY ON THE REAR. A LOOK OF INDIGNATION, EMMA LUNGES BACK INTO THE ATTACK. STEED RISES FROM CHAIR. THEY CONTINUE COMBAT.
STEED: Why not? We can build sandcastles together.
EMMA: I refuse to carry your bucket and spade.
STEED: Brisk walks along... along the seashore... sand beneath your feet. The breeze snatching at your hair. (PARRY. THRUST. PARRY. STEED SIDE-STEPS ATTACK, EMMA BECOMES ENTWINED IN WINDOW CURTAINS.) Have you ever fancied yourself as a schoolteacher?
EMMA SURFACES
EMMA (BEAT): That was very, very dirty.
STEED EMERGES FROM THE KITCHEN, MILK JUG IN HAND.
STEED (SMILES): You're quite right... but I didn't promise to fight fair. No worry about driving, we'll take the train.
EMMA: When did you buy the tickets?
STEED: *Yesterday morning.* We'll have to hurry... the train leaves in less than an hour. I'll explain the details to you on the way down.
EMMA (RESIGNED): And where are *we* going?
STEED: Little-Bazeley-by-the-Sea.

Beautifully played, it's painful to see again after all this time, partly because of how slim one is, but also to see my stunt double Rocky Taylor crossing swords with Diana. (Did you think it was *me*?)

That glorious little tap across the bottom gives the scene an extra touch of class. (A Clemens trademark.) That's what got to people. The fact that her clothes were revealing, interesting, but worn. As Brian Clemens has said, it shows real vulnerability. She's not a hard, tough, dominant woman, that's the whole point — she is funny, sweet and adorable. Diana brushing the hair out of her eyes and the lovely moment when I wrap her up in the curtain and out she comes are wonderful! ∎

was seen as the one with the personality, the one with the shock values, the one with a sense of fun. But I wasn't prepared. I hadn't tried this character out on film. I'd just skated into it when we did the 'as live' shows and it had been easy in a way, since I just went through it as myself.

So when it came to doing this scene, I said, "*She* should play the tuba, not me!"

They insisted, "But Pat, you're the lead in the show, she's your assistant."

I shook my head. "No. She's my *partner*!"

They considered this and agreed to try it. Di and I played the scene. It worked, because besides being one of the great classical actresses, as she now is — Dame Diana Rigg — she is, and always was, a delightful comedienne.

The memory of Diana playing the tuba, that morning in Steed's apartment, makes me laugh, even today after thirty years. (She's also great with a foil, a scythe, a broadsword and does a mean Dance of the Seven Veils!)

After about a month of filming, I married Kate and went off on honeymoon to Tunisia. It was obvious from the start that the marriage was a disaster. It dawned on me then that I was wedded not to Kate, but for better or for worse, I was married to the show.

I rented a car and drove at ninety miles an hour, as if my life depended on it, from our honeymoon haven in southern Tunisia back to *The Avengers*.

I returned to the film set and got very excited because, suddenly, Di Rigg and I made tremendous sense. I remember that I drove her up to Norfolk, to re-film scenes for the aborted Beth Shepherd episode. We drove there in my newly-acquired Jaguar saloon. We discovered then that we had very much the same sense of humour and I quickly developed a great fondness for her. We hit it off right away, without saying anything but simply by being in each other's company. I'd reached out to her and she touched me with kindness and companionship.

I was always — well, most of the time — submissive with Honor Blackman. She was always in charge, and I think I did what I did rather well, except that I always abjured what I did to *her*, the woman in the show. I did it naturally. As she told me later, "Sean Connery wouldn't let me get away with anything", implying that I always did, and, of course, I had.

Honor would be the first to deny that she had things all her own way, because she didn't, really. The two of us were equals. We were never jealous of each other, but I know that I had a deep streak of envy running through my veins, because during our time together she had an enormous amount of publicity. Honor was in every newspaper, *constantly*. I didn't

Above: One liked to touch on sexual perversions and bring in things like leather, rubber and tying-up.

Left: A sequence that might have been filmed with Cathy Gale, but was too complicated to produce live in the studio.

Above: Diana designed this costume herself — and the flak came fast and furious, resulting in the episode 'A Touch of Brimstone' being banned in America!

Right: 'A Sense of History'.

begrudge her that, though. She was wonderful with publicity and we had lots of fun working together — a pleasure that continued with Diana.

Di would come onto the set and we would relish working together. We danced and we fought, playfully throwing things at each other. We talked, we invented lines — well, not exactly lines because Brian Clemens had written them, and they were good — but we always wanted to change things, to spark things up, to do things for no reason, for the *opposite* reason. I've always been an iconoclast. I still am, even more so now that I'm an old man. I say what I think, so we enjoyed doing it quite differently from the way that everybody else did it.

One liked to touch on sexual perversions and bring in things like leather, rubber and tying-up. That appealed to me and I think we put that in *The Avengers*... well, we *suggested* it, which was great fun.

In one show, 'A Touch of Brimstone' — considered *too* kinky for America, where it was banned — Diana played a Sin Queen dressed in a whalebone corset, high, laced boots and a spiked dog collar. The scenes also offended the normally permissive British TV officials. A thirty-eight second sequence in which Di was whipped by the villain was cut.

"We're constantly kinky," one of the producers told the American press. "If there's a choice between Emma Peel fighting in a wet dress or a dry one, we choose wet. In addition, she likes to wear leather clothing, knows judo and often takes on six men at once."

I loved all that.

I'm the first to admit it — I was a very kinky man. If you come from a public school background, you grow up with the association of pain and off-beat-type approaches to sex. So consequently I was brought up in that range. I was brought up surrounded by a lot of strange women, and this made me the ideal *man* to make a series with these *women*, because nothing they did surprised me. The most important aspect of the way I played Steed was in *reaction*, not action.

I had a little bit of action, of course, but I was very unathletic and I did as little as I possibly could. But my *reaction* to the many crazy characters in *The Avengers* set them off into more and more outrageous excitement, because I didn't impinge on their territory — I didn't stop them from pursuing their own devices. I was able to *listen* to what their madness or their eccentricity provided. You'll see this over and over again in the show, a good example being the railway carriage scene with Ronald Fraser in 'The Gravediggers'. Note that I, in fact, don't do anything but respond to him with a nod, a smile, a glance and ask if I can close the window or something, in a sequence that runs to six minutes!

That was the trick of the way we played the show. I was the straight man to the women's role of activator. That's what made the show so entertaining, because you expected me, the man, to make the decisions and I didn't. The women did.

One of the reasons why actors liked coming on the show was that all these parts, whether they were eccentrics or heavies, were always exciting. They were always played brilliantly because the actors knew that they wouldn't be trampled on by me or, indeed, by my female partners. We played *to* these people, never ever against them. And yet, one was required to have the grace and manners of a gentleman but underneath to be steel, which is what I tried to convey with Steed.

What Diana achieved as Emma is beautifully summed up by **Peter Graham Scott**:

'Diana took to the part amazingly well. I remember that when she played her first scene with Patrick Cargill (no mean actor himself) in 'The Murder Market', he was amazed, because she was throwing him lines like, "Well, *what*

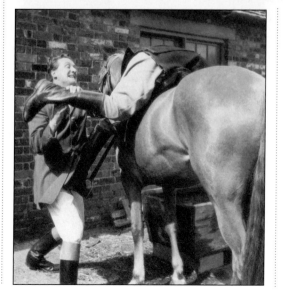

I did as little of the action as I possibly could. Nevertheless there were times when Steed found himself in the thick of battle.
From top to bottom: the duel with Frant (Jeremy Young) in 'A Touch of Brimstone'; in 'The Murder Market' Lovejoy (Patrick Cargill) has his knuckles rapped by Steed; Steed saddles one of Omrod's thugs in 'Silent Dust'.

With Ronald Fraser at Stableford Park, Melton Mowbray in Leicestershire, the location of the famous miniature railway.

ing with a long scene, the intricacies of the plot or whatever, was to take a deep breath and belt it out in a very high-pitched voice, which of course is the opposite of what she does now. (She's got the most beautiful voice in the world.) At that time she would think, "Oh, it's a long speech," and her words would come tumbling out so fast that you could never hear a thing. Then she'd flick back her hair and walk out of the door. My way was the direct opposite. I would speak *frightfully slowly* and walk around a lot while I was getting the speech out.

I'd been taught way back that the best way to emphasise a point was to start walking and talking at the same time, then stop or sit down *on* the second syllable of the word of dialogue, not between. So, if one was saying 'create' (a two syllable word), one would sit down on 'ate'— the second syllable. By doing this you'd made your point, then you'd get up again when it was time to make another point, also *on* the syllable, not between. It was a very simplistic way of acting, but it worked... for me. But then I didn't really have 'spark', except in close-ups, or when I felt that I'd been wronged in some way. Also, I didn't walk all that stylishly. Roger Moore said to me recently, when we were at a party and he saw me walking away, "My God, Macnee, there's that butch walk again."

One had to do this and hit one's mark, which was not always easy.

Director **Charles Crichton** (who directed many of the Ealing comedies, and would go on to be nominated for an Oscar for *A Fish Called Wanda*) expounds:

'While I enjoyed working with Patrick and Diana on good scripts, they may not have enjoyed working with *me*, because I had become obsessed by the zoom lens.

'The zoom lens, I thought, would give the actors freedom. We would be able to shoot pages and pages of script without cutting and interrupting the flow of their talent. It did not quite work that way. There were soon dozens of marks all over the set, which they had to hit with pinpoint accuracy. One inch to the left or one to the right and it was no good for the lights and no good for the camera. I put them both in a horrible situation, but the flow of their talent survived.'

By now, Brian Clemens had gathered together a marvellous school of writers, who I thought were awfully good and had to be, to quote Brian, "*Avengers*-minded."

I should have been "*Avengers*-minded" too, but I didn't, at any time, really understand what that meant. Nobody told me how I

exactly have you got in mind?" with such innuendo that he was flummoxed. He'd never had an actress coming on to him like that before. The lines were written, of course, it was simply the way that Diana projected them. He did an immediate reaction and I said, "Patrick, we really must keep that in."'

One did these things on instinct, of course. I came from that background, so I was able to wear the clothes and speak in that certain way. I had a training in classical theatre so I knew how to pronounce my consonants. Then, when I came to act with Diana Rigg, who had the consummate, natural assertion of someone who had already played the big parts in Shakespeare, I just felt awfully good with her from the first time we met.

I needed a lot of application to learn my lines, to express my thought, to do whatever was needed. She didn't, because the work she was doing with me was, to her, low on the scale, *easy* for her to assimilate.

Not surprisingly, Diana was nervous in the early stages. I remember that her way of cop-

should play Steed, or relate to other people. I never, ever, got a brief. It was never written down. The script for 'Hot Snow', the first episode in December 1960, said:

'Keel is about to push the bell button when the door is flung open. *Steed stands there.*'

Just that, nothing else. No description. Nothing. So I just made him up. The added threat of instant dismissal three weeks later enabled me to create him myself, *very quickly*. But it was never, ever written down. And now, with the planned *Avengers* film, there will be somebody else playing him, as if he were a properly defined character. Steed was never that. He was never a character in literature, like Bulldog Drummond, Simon Templar or James Bond, or a persona somebody else had first created in another medium. Steed was never written down — 'Steed stands there' — and I was the man. I'm awfully proud of that. As time went on, Steed and myself just grew together. I played it how I was feeling on that particular day, which worked in a funny kind of way, because the whole point of the show was that it was immediate. So my thinking,

which was reasonably intelligent, was to tune it to the social mores of the time. Being born Aquarian made me feel, always, slightly *ahead* of my time.

I just knew that the women wouldn't stand for any nonsense. They always seemed to be looking upon me and saying, "Oh, come along, Patrick. Really!" — which in a way was good, because one had a completely androgynous approach to things, which once again, was very fashionable at that time. Nobody wanted to be overtly sexual, they wanted to be quietly perverse. I represented that and I represented it in good old fashioned English form.

At that time, neither Diana nor I realised that we were making history, and producing twenty-six episodes of what are probably, of their genre, the best black and white shows that have been produced for television. They are still the *classic Avengers* episodes, the ones that really matter.

————

Near to the end of filming, Brian Clemens arranged for Herb Rosenthal, the programme buyer for ABC in America, to view a fine print

'Death at Bargain Prices'.

of the episode 'The Town of No Return'. A short time later we were told that the show had been bought by Tom Moore, head of the ABC network in New York. *The Avengers* was to open in the United States on 28 March 1965 — the first network sale to the USA by any British television company.

In April 1965, Diana and I flew to America to promote it, in the company of Bob Norris, an American who handled ABPC's overseas sales.

We stayed next to each other in the St Moritz Hotel, New York. The entire Stratford Memorial Theatre cast of *Marat de Sade* was there, including Glenda Jackson, who had taken over Di's role as Charlotte Corday in the show when Di left to join *The Avengers*. We laughed about this and enjoyed ourselves, then went on appearances to promote our ridiculous show about "the man with the umbrella and the woman who throws men over her shoulder," as one American critic dubbed us!

From New York we did a four city tour of Chicago, Boston, Philadelphia and Washington. Everywhere we went, we did interviews literally around the clock, explaining what the characters and the show were about. Di wasn't used to this sort of thing and sometimes asked me if I'd mind doing them by myself. I was happy to, but Bob Norris requested that we did all the interviews together.

We met countless top American executives, dozens and dozens of people, so Di and I were seldom apart. The way that we promoted it was extraordinary. Publicly, we were awfully good together — quite a couple, in fact.

Attending one of these junkets, at a fashionable New York mid-town restaurant, Di turned up attired in her John Bates-designed form-fitting jersey slacks and was refused admission until she changed into a skirt! "Oh, well," she shrugged, "I hope they aren't as fussy elsewhere."

We then visited Canada, where the series was already running with great success. Towards the end Di asked me what I was going to do during the time we had left. I said, "I think I'll go to the West Coast of America, see my friends and ask my wife to join me."

She said, "Good luck. Have fun." I kissed her on the cheek and left her in New York.

Stefanie Powers had lent us a house for two weeks in Malibu and Kate joined me there. It was then that I was asked to appear in the play *There's a Girl in My Soup*. I turned it down. I also got rid of my lovely agent Richard Hatton, who'd negotiated me the golden two and a half per cent profit share of *The Avengers* in 1964. I let Richard go and changed to the William Morris Agency. I left them shortly afterwards and joined Jean Diamond. Then I fell out with her and went back to the Morris people. During that time Kate got to know all of my friends in California, and met a neuro-surgeon. On the last day of our holiday, she arrived with this chap and told me she was leaving me for him — at the same time, she was also very pleased that my son Rupert had been accepted at Princeton! (So was I. From England that was quite an achievement.) Devastated, I returned to England and plunged into the depths of despair.

I should have divorced her right away, of course, but I didn't. I bit the bullet and threw myself into my work.

One of the things I did was *The Lady's Not for Burning* with Barbara Jefford, which I'd previously played to great success in Canada. This time I had bouts of anxiety during rehearsals and dried several times, because I couldn't get away from the thought that Kate had left me.

From that I went into a play in the television series *Love Story*, with Hannah Gordon. Wonderfully written by Alfred Shaughnessy, who was later the script editor of *Upstairs, Downstairs*, I played a film star and Hannah was a typist who wins an evening out with me as a prize in a crossword puzzle competition. Hannah was lovely. We played it beautifully.

Then I went off and spent three weeks with a girl who played an extra in the show. Perfectly gorgeous, she was blonde, buxom and had a sweet, open smile. I asked her if she'd come along with me to southern Spain. She gave me an enthusiastic nod and I went to pick her up in my Jaguar, which I'd bought the year before for the huge sum of £2,000.

Her pride and joy was an open top Baby Austin with bucket seats — a fine-looking little car — which she elected to drive down through the whole of Spain, the Jaguar being too dashing. Driving at fast speed and squeaking the klaxon horn as she zipped around corners, she attracted an enormous amount of attention. It was wonderful. I felt a lot better after that and I like to think that she did, too.

Then Di came to see me and said she couldn't take it any more. "I've had enough. *I'm not coming back!"*

Diana had always given me the impression, slightly, that she really wished she was somewhere else. At the time, I couldn't understand why. Now I know. Her only friend was her chauffeur!

I didn't realise that she was being treated really badly in terms of pay, or in terms of the way that 'they', the executives at ABPC, looked after her. I didn't know any of this. I assumed that all was lovely with her because *I* thought that all was lovely with her.

Towards the end of 1965, an article ran in the newspapers saying that she was unhappy. Di actually went into print to say that she was

Above: With actress Barbara Jefford in The Lady's Not For Burning (ATV 1966).

Left: My Jaguar, which cost the huge sum of £2,000.

Opposite above: Celebrating the sale of The Avengers to America — with champagne, of course.

Opposite below: Pictured at London Airport prior to departure to New York for a four-city tour to promote the show in America.

receiving the same amount of money as a coal miner. "I want more!" (As a result, there were several derisive letters to the newspapers from disgruntled coal miners!)

She didn't get anywhere until she threatened to leave. Then they said, "Oh, you can't do that!"

"Why not?" she asked.

"Because..." they threatened. She was under contract.

"No, not *because*," said Di. "Give me a proper wage and I'll stay."

She was absolutely right to do this. She was probably the best exponent of Stoppard, of Shakespeare, the Greek tragedies — even light comedy. There was no limit to her talent, and here she was working for meagre rates of pay. I think, at the time, ABPC didn't know what they had.

Albert Fennell was very nice to her. She loved Albert because he took the trouble to be pleasant. She got along well with Brian Clemens, but he was far too busy trying to keep to the filming schedule to form a close relationship with Diana. She was fond of Laurie Johnson, who would pop into the studio, chat for a short time, then disappear to compose another evocative score. The crew were

very fond of her, but her only friend was her chauffeur and confidant, John Taylor!

A cloud engulfed me — a thick, dark impenetrable gloom — and I was so taken with my own problems that I couldn't face up to hers. What I should have said was, "Don't be so ridiculous, Diana. We've got ourselves an enormous hit here, we *have* to go to a second season."

I didn't. I didn't take her out to dinner to chat about her concerns. I didn't sit down and listen to her. I just felt sad. Sad for Diana and sorry for myself.

Now I realise that it *was* up to me to persuade Diana to stay. I was happy with her and she was happy with me, professionally, because we made it all work. But I ignored her anxiety and pain. I still carry the guilt that I didn't pay more attention to her then, or later, when the crunch came.

It was about this time that I met Honor Blackman again, who accurately told me that I needed psychological help, advice which I took. I began to see things a little more clearly, but I still couldn't get Kate out of my head.

It took a long time for the Diana Rigg shows to come out. When they did, she came in for some awful stick from the media.

Diana and myself pictured with Howard Thomas outside Elstree Studios during the making of season four.

It was, "Oh, this girl's a drag. She's nothing like Honor Blackman." Then, of course, when the viewers accepted her as the new *Avengers* girl, the critics started to appreciate what she'd brought with her: this gorgeous creature in the tight leather jump-suits, the clearly delineated body movements of her classical training at Stratford, her experience of life which came to bear with a flash of her eyes which said, "I'm an intellect. I *mean* something. I'm red-headed and I'm Yorkshire, and *nothing is going to stand in my way*!" And nothing did, despite the fact that Diana, as Emma, was asked to do things that were alien to her.

Early during the production, I remember that I asked Brian Clemens if we could make an episode which would enable me to show that I could ride a horse.

Some time later, I was presented with a wonderful script written by Roger Marshall, 'Silent Dust', about fox-hunting and dubious practices among the landed gentry. Steed and Emma would round up the miscreants on horseback, in true-blooded Western hero style.

On the day of shooting, I was provided with the horse which Laurence Olivier had ridden in his film *Henry V*, in the sequence when he reared the horse onto its hind legs and roared out the line, "Once more unto the breach, dear friends!" The horse was then two years old.

Twenty years later, at twenty-two, I had him standing on his hind legs again, and rode him for several days. He was wonderful.

Di Rigg also had a horse.

She turned up in the morning for her riding scene, dressed in a beautiful riding coat, a black bowler hat, a cravat with a pin in it and riding breeches.

"Where's my horse?" she asked.

They gave it to her. She sat in the saddle and

Harry Pottle

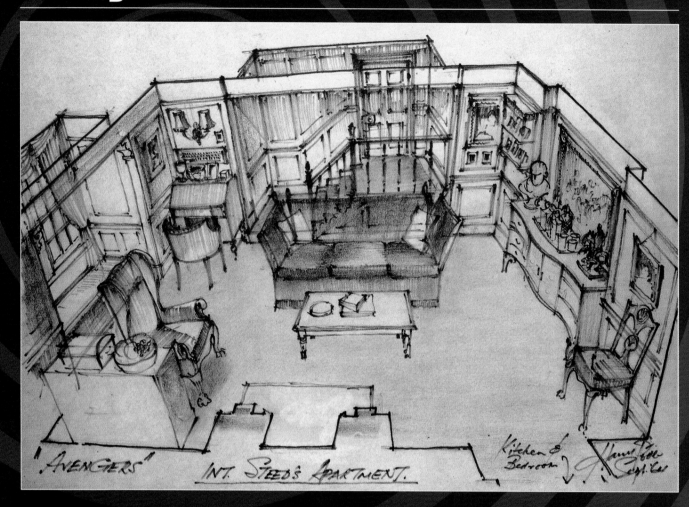

"AVENGERS" INT. STEED'S APARTMENT. Kitchen & Bedroom

Art designer Harry Pottle's remarkable sets were artistically important to the success of the monochrome shows, pushing the boundaries of design for a television show to the limit. He describes how they were created:

I was given a free hand when designing the sets. Not knowing what the scripts for future episodes might require, I decided on a flexible, contemporary sixties set for Emma, which would contrast well with Steed's panelled set with its military background.

The set was octagonal with two recessed walls, material-covered sliding doors leading to the kitchen and bedroom, a window wall with a door leading out onto the terrace (a roof top panorama painted backcloth) and a wall with an entrance door. There was a central hooded stove and a built-in seating unit. One recess had a drinks cabinet with a top that slid aside and up came the glasses and drinks on a counter-balance lift. The walls were easily moved out to make the set open-sided for ease of shooting. The lighting gantry remained permanently in place.

Steed's apartment had its entrance doorway on a landing and came complete with a handrail and a short flight of steps leading down into the main living area. Atmosphere was created with its furnishings and military memorabilia, enhancing Steed's character as the elegant, suave, ex-military gentleman, and the apartment reflected 'club'-style comfort and good taste.

Once the series started shooting, each episode took ten to twelve days to film, with an average of ten sets. While one was in use, the next was being pre-fabricated in the workshops, to be moved onto the stage as shooting finished on a set and the space became available. Meanwhile, I was designing the sets for the following show, the working drawings being done by Denise Exshaw.

The sequence was: one set being filmed, one being built and one designed. The directors had two weeks to prepare their episode, so the sets were already designed, drawn and being built when they arrived. We would run through the script and the sketches and very rarely did they ask for modifications.

Each episode seemed to have one set

Harry Pottle's original design sketches for Steed's apartment (left), the dance studio (above right) and Mrs Peel's apartment (below right).

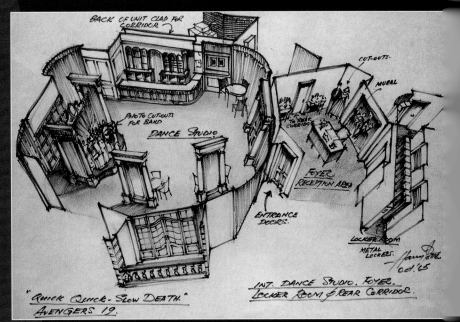

"*QUICK QUICK-SLOW DEATH.*"
AVENGERS 19.

INT. DANCE STUDIO. FOYER.
LOCKER ROOM & REAR CORRIDOR.

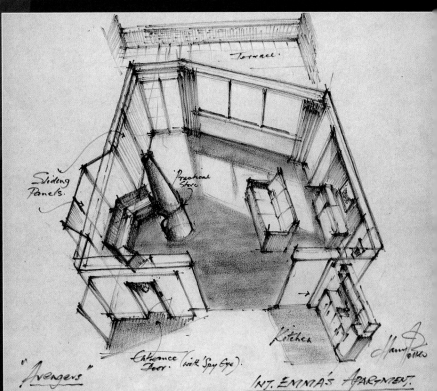

"*Avengers*"

INT. EMMA'S APARTMENT.

that would be fun to design, either by being able to go O.T.T. or designed in simplistic terms with the barest essentials to create the required background.

The karate school in 'The Cybernauts', for instance, was just a black floor with black drapes for walls, ornate entrance doors and a large red and gold Chinese gong. All the actors wore white karate costumes.

In the dance room set for 'A Quick-Quick Slow Death', I used the Victor Sylvester *How to Dance* primer book for the footprints across the floor and up the wall. Pat just followed them across the room, tripping the light-fantastic!

The dating agency set for 'The Murder Market' was in candyfloss pink and white, with cake doilies serving as silver decoration — a bit of a Niagara Falls honeymoon suite send-up.

In 'Death at Bargain Prices' the threat was a bomb in the base of a lift shaft. The only lift in the studio was in the electrical store, and that only went up one floor. By careful re-dressing for each landing, director Charles Crichton was able to create tension and the impression of a multi-storey department store.

For 'The Man-Eater of Surrey Green' we needed a huge tendril with which to threaten Mrs Peel. It's amazing what one can achieve with a prop-room snake. Stick needle spines all over it, spray it green — a man-eater!

The problem with 'The House That Jack Built' was designing a set with the minimum amount of building that would create the illusion that one always ended up at the same point. I designed it with a central area of the floor painted with concentric circular bands which narrowed to the centre, giving the floor a domed appearance. The walls were trellised arches with four perspectives and one long corridor, with a zig-zag pattern on the floor and an interchangeable door or window at the end. The trellis arches were evenly spaced down its length. One side had a solid wall with applied cut-out shapes like brambles, and the other side was gauze with cut-out shapes. The gauze

became solid when front-lit and transparent when back-lit, which meant that the camera could track with the artiste down either side of the corridor or outside, with the shapes on the gauze in the foreground adding to the menace.

Although all twenty-six episodes I designed were filmed in black and white, all the sets were painted in colours, which I believe created a better

mood for the actors rather than everything being in 'tech greys', as was the practice at that time.

When Harry left us at the end of the season, to join Eon Productions to work on the Bond movie *You Only Live Twice* (directed by my good friend Lewis Gilbert), I couldn't help thinking that our loss was Bond's gain. ■

In 'Silent Dust', with the same horse Laurence Olivier had ridden in Henry V, *twenty years earlier.*

did the scenes where Emma Peel is running to the hounds and eventually falls off after having a fight with the villainess of the piece. (A lot of this was done by the stunt people, of course. Ray Austin doubled Diana during the fall, and was knocked unconscious for five minutes when he fell into a hole!)

Then both of us were called upon to shoot tracking shots. We cantered across the field and I suddenly realised that Diana had never been on a horse before in her life!

"Do you ride?" I asked.

She shook her head. "Not until the day before yesterday."

"What did you do the day before yesterday?" I enquired.

She smiled. "I went and had a lesson!"

I was stunned.

When we dismounted after the scenes were done, she looked a little drawn, a little pale, a little tense — but she'd done it! That was typical of Di. "Here we go…" She just had that sublime, simple courage.

Little wonder that the executives from ABC

TV in America loved what they saw, and that she became the darling of everybody. However, the show still had to prove itself to American audiences… and critics.

The morning after the show's American début, the critics published their reviews. Most liked us, but not everyone.

'A brutal British import with tongue-in-cheek humour,' was one comment. 'None of the flair of *The Man from U.N.C.L.E.*,' was another. 'The American Broadcasting Company, whose stated intention is "to bring as much newness and variety to the summer television schedule as we possibly can," last night unveiled *The Avengers*, a British-made, hour-long, tongue-in-cheek secret agent series,' wrote Vincent Canby, of the *New York Times*. '*ABC is obviously pulling our leg!* [My italics.] The weekly series suffers in its American début by comparison with so many other, locally familiar shows that mix mayhem, mystery and comedy in approximately the same predictable proportions.

'The faces on *The Avengers* are new and attrac-

Above: Diana cantered across the field – and I suddenly realised that she had never been on a horse before in her life!

Left: A rose by any other name...

Things were different in England.

'Last Friday night's edition of *The Avengers* was vintage stuff,' wrote the critic for *The Stage and Television Today*. 'Just lately I thought the series had been losing its flair for the exotic and the absurd. An unwanted touch of scientific realism had even entered with white coated villains plotting away in laboratories. However, Brian Clemens' 'A Touch of Brimstone' had just the right mixture of extravagance and menace.

'The opening was riveting. An armchair backed threateningly towards the camera, swivelled round and was seen to contain Peter Wyngarde at his most aristocratic. He switched on a television set and laid out his liqueur chocolates with great care while a bulky figure on the screen talked about Anglo-Russian relations. He watched with amusement as the man selected a cigar from a conveniently placed case. We saw the reason for his amusement when, as the man's argument reached its height, the joke cigar suddenly exploded.

'This was the prelude to a plot about an attempt by the Hellfire Club — modelled on the famous eighteenth century band of rakehells — to embarrass the Government before staging a brisk *coup d'état*. Preposterous? Of course. But what mattered was that the villains behaved as if they took it all seriously while Steed was able to point out the ludicrousness of the situation. "Follow that chair!" he cried, as the sedan chair packed with explosives flittered past at the Hellfire Club's annual rave-up. Earlier on he had explained to a shaken aristocrat his patent hangover cure, "National Anthem. It soon gets you to your feet."

'Brian Clemens' script was full of throwaway quips of this nature. At the same time, it managed to convey a strong sense of impending danger at certain moments — as when masked figures encircled a gentleman who, rather unsportingly, wished to register a complaint against the Club. James Hill's direction was also deft and came close to accomplishing the difficult task of making an orgy look convincing.

'Patrick Macnee's Steed is by now unimprovable. One's only regret is that he has not had more chance to exploit his comic timing and thoroughbred appearance outside this particular series. Opinions about Diana Rigg's performance are divided. I feel that she had made a definable character of Emma Peel, something without much help from the scriptwriters. And whatever her costumes — last week she was a strikingly clad Queen of Sin — she has looked constantly fetching.'

The Times of London hailed 'the wonderfully good-chap sexuality of it all,' and Jonathan Miller, the doctor/actor/director/social critic, told the media that he loved the 'absolute

tive,' he continued, 'belonging to Patrick Macnee, as agent John Steed, and Diana Rigg, as Mrs Emma Peel, his assistant who is also, apparently, a widow of some means. However, no amount of 1966 dialogue about automation and transistors can obscure the fact that the formula was discovered during radio's early iron age, before showbusiness alchemists had turned Mike Hammer into the solid-gold James Bond.'

Mr Canby felt that it was never made clear whether Steed was a comparatively parochial private eye or a government agent with an international beat. 'It is the lack of such a fact that prevents a guy from really being able to identify.' (Oddly enough, Vincent Canby went on to become one of the show's biggest champions.)

unreality, violence, symbolism, magic, masques, sex, change — everything that excites the imagination and senses. Any show that has all this is unique.'

The nucleus for those unique storylines could germinate from any source, as **Roger Marshall** unfolds:

'I went with Brian Clemens to the first location shoot in Norfolk (for 'The Town of No Return'). While there, we came across an old RAF airfield which was being kept in mothballs. As we trudged the long deserted runways and went up into the control tower, overrun by a flock of starlings, we both got the same idea: an entire episode shot on this very location. With creativity at full throttle, we plotted the broad strokes of the story on the car journey back to London. Steed would be taking Emma to 'RAF Hamelin' for a reunion party. It was one of the bases from which he flew during the 'white rabbit' phase of his active service career. Gerry O'Hara was set to direct. It would take more than Steed and Emma Peel to throw the man who cured Glenn Ford's dandruff! Unlike some of his rivals, Gerry's skill and ingenuity hadn't been blunted by years of toil on all those awful mid-Atlantic schlock operas which, properly derided at the time, are now miraculously hailed as 'cult television'.

'Gerry did his recce, saw the very huts and hangars that Brian and I had seen, and was all ready to say, "Action." It was then that the number crunchers at ABPC — our partners — played their ace: "No Norfolk... too expensive... find somewhere local." He did and, despite the Scottish mafia, 'The Hour That Never Was' got made. Twenty years on, Milton Shulman still remembered it, in his *Evening Standard* column, as his favourite episode. What tickled him was the notion that a dentist could imagine he'd take over the world with the sound of his high speed drill. Nothing remarkable about that; a perfectly standard *Avengers* conceit. At the time Pat Macnee said it was the episode that turned the series round in the States. I don't know about that, but it worked largely because it was directed by a man who really knew film and was shot within the confines of one deserted airfield. Disbelief was suspended at the perimeter gate. Without the imaginative input from the set designers, we sometimes struggled to find believable locations for Steed and Emma to work in — Borehamwood High Street and Steed's vintage Bentley did not make ideal bed-fellows.'

By now our ratings and popularity had soared in America, earning the show an emphatic

'The Girl From Auntie'.

expression of approval from many of the most prestigious US newspapers and magazines.

Cleveland Amory, critic for the American TV listings magazine, *TV Guide*, wrote: 'Together Mr Steed and Mrs Peel, who never call each other anything but that, are a pair. At one point Mr Steed comes bursting in to tell Mrs Peel that he has been murderously attacked by a savage. "Fortunately," he says, "he overlooked my cucumber sandwiches." "Oh," says Mrs Peel, taking one, "good." Such scenes stick to your ribs, they do.'

I knew what he meant. Di and I certainly had fun playing them, and would prosper anew. We were about to take our next step — *The Avengers* was going to be filmed in colour! But would Diana still be with us? ■

Seldom has a man earned his gratuity, or showed such determination to the cause, as the ABPC executive assigned by Howard Thomas to try and persuade Diana not to leave the show. For several weeks, he followed her around the studio like a Mother Hen marshalling a chick. He wined her, he dined her and made (ambitious) claims that the second series would be an even bigger success than the first. Bouquets of flowers were delivered to Diana's dressing room — from the executive.

After protracted discussions with ABPC, her agent negotiated a new contract. Apparently ABPC had agreed that the shooting schedule for the colour series would begin at such time as to allow Diana to complete her commitment with the Royal Shakespeare Company at Stratford. She would be allowed to leave the studios at 10.30am on matinee days, in order to get to Stratford comfortably for the afternoon performance. Transport would be provided by the studio to take her to and from Elstree. Her new wardrobe for the series should be designed and completed *before* filming began. (Prior to the arrival of John Bates and Jean Muir, several weeks into the filming of the monochrome episodes, her wardrobe for the series had arrived in dribs and drabs.)

Aware that ABPC were committed to hand-over dates with the ABC network in America and there wasn't time to recast, her agent had negotiated an increase of Diana's salary and, the knock-out punch, a small percentage share of the profits!

Throughout all this, I'd been working for Lew Grade's ATV network in the *Love Story* show with Hannah Gordon, waiting to hear if the colour series was really going to happen. That it was, and Diana was staying, made me very happy indeed.

Shooting on the new series — the first in colour, the second on film, the fifth in all — began on Monday 5 September, on location at Palace House, Hampshire, the home of Lord Montague of Beaulieu.

We spent two glorious days there, filming sequences with selected vehicles from Lord Montague's Museum of Vintage Cars, the idea being to shoot sequences that were to be used as 'tag' scenes in the forthcoming episodes. In the previous season, each episode had ended with Emma and Steed riding off in some form

of transport — a rickshaw, a balloon, a tandem cycle, etc. This time, we would drive off each week from Palace House in a different vintage car, with some suitable comedy gimmick involved, the vignettes being created by Brian Clemens, who joined us there. Incidentally, the fact that I drove the Bentley and couldn't change out of third gear and had to start from the top of a hill or be pushed into view by studio technicians, is neither here nor there. It went and they'd speed up the film — the most important fact being that Steed *drove* a Bentley, or a Rolls, what have you. (People loved the old classic cars, but I didn't know anything about them at all... I didn't even know that one had to double de-clutch! But I

Opposite: White horse. White catsuit. Diana, on location at Woburn Sands.

INTO COLOUR

Right: Filming a sequence with a veteran vehicle from Lord Montague's Museum of Vintage Cars.

Below: Filming the colour series on location at Palace House, Hampshire.

drove one, that's what mattered. However, I think that the change to the vintage Rolls Royce, in the later shows, was a mistake. It was pretentious, whereas the Bentley was in keeping with Steed's character — his correctness. He wouldn't have been so ostentatious as to have had a Rolls.)

For this season, we really went to town. Diana and I visited Pierre Cardin, the top fashion designer, who agreed to design our wardrobes. We met him in Paris, at his fashion show. Towards the end of it, he suddenly collapsed and was carried out by four strong men. I was stunned, but apparently it had happened before.

Before the show, I'd been introduced to his lady colleague, who gave me the impression that she would very much like me to become associated with the company. At that time I was quite proud of my wardrobe, in the sense that the clothes I wore as Steed had been designed by me. I didn't really *design* them, of course, I just said how I'd like this, how I'd like that, and the wardrobe people passed my ideas along to the tailor. But I *felt* that I'd designed them — that is what happens when one is appearing in a long-running series, you begin to think that you can be a doctor, or a lawyer, or a policeman, when in fact you're still just an actor. I had a bad case of that, despite pretending I didn't. Incidentally, Di's clothes from Pierre Cardin were delayed, owing to the August showing of the Paris couture, so her wardrobe was augmented by a number of items from a young theatrical designer called Alan Hughes, who continued to design her *Avengers* outfits. I also had a beautiful, plum-coloured evening suit, with a fabulous gold brocade waistcoat, designed by Hardy Amies, who also offered me a tie-up.

I never did sign a deal with Cardin or Amies, because Julian Wintle inferred that I wasn't allowed to undertake any 'outside activities'. Television commercials were also a no-no.

I remember that I was offered a Schweppes commercial and turned it down without even considering it, leaving the way open for "You know who" — Bill Franklyn — to do extremely well. I could have done that so perfectly with my bowler and umbrella.

What I didn't realise at the time was that ABPC had decided nobody connected with *The Avengers* could do commercials, because it was felt it would cheapen the show. (That things changed later, and both Diana and Linda Thorson were allowed to appear in television commercials for soap and hair colourants respectively, did my pocketbook no good at all, at least not then. I finally did one, with Philip Saville, which paid very nicely.)

Diana and I put a tremendous amount of inspiration into the colour series — probably too much, it certainly didn't bring *me* any plaudits. I remember *Playboy* magazine coming out with a review of the colour shows which read, 'Well the man doesn't *mean* anything, but the girl is just sensational!', and went into a long description of Diana's attributes... which was right, of course.

This was in May 1967, when the show was nominated in two categories for the Emmy awards; *The Avengers* for the year's Outstanding Dramatic Series and Diana for the Outstanding Continued Performance by an Actress in a Leading Role in a Dramatic Series.

The awards were to be announced in New York on Sunday 4 June. The company gave us three days off, and we flew out on Pan American Flight 103 at 3.00pm on the Saturday — the richer by the $100 we'd been given by the company as 'incidental expenditure'!

I had an awful feeling as I sat beside Diana.

Above: At Palace House, Beaulieu, filming the colour season teasers.

Above: This picture (in colour) adorned the front cover of the American TV listings magazine TV Guide. *I was so proud.*

Right: About to leave London Airport for New York. The occasion: Diana and The Avengers *had been nominated for an Emmy award.*

Opposite above: With Christopher Lee on the set of the episode 'Never, Never Say Die'. We're looking at our old school photo!

I was longing for her to win the leading actress award, of course, but at the same time feeling miserable that *I* hadn't even been nominated.

The Avengers was beaten by *Mission Impossible* in both categories, Barbara Bain beating Diana for the leading actress award. Barbara *who?* Whatever happened to Barbara Bain? We now have *Dame* Diana! There again, I suppose one could ask, "Whatever happened to Pat Macnee?" Well, he apparently didn't deserve an Emmy. But then I rarely got good reviews, because I was always looked upon in comparison with the women. This hurt me, of course, but I had a strange ego of my own which drove me on. I was constant in my loyalty to the show.

After the awards ceremony, it was back to the studio for many more weeks of alternately hilarious and piquant routine.

What I found so extraordinary was, despite the injection of many thousands of pounds, and the acknowledged expertise of the Wintle team, the board at ABPC never warmed to the idea of having colour from day one. It's a matter of record that Julian, Albert and Brian wanted to go into colour as early as mid way through the black and white shows. The executives were having none of it.

The majority of people at ABPC were rather tentative. They had a blinkered attitude that said, "We know best." Nobody talked to us, and when they did so, it was always in a rush because they wanted us to move forwards, to get back to work. Had they offered us a little bit of humanity, understanding and trust as actors, got us in there and told *us* what *they* were trying to do, life for all of us — including the producers — would have been a joy. That's how it should have been, not this "Oh, we mustn't get too pally. You know what *actors* are like!" attitude. Actors are not like that — whatever *that* may be! Actors are human beings, with feelings. They didn't appear to think so. They certainly didn't *pay* us like human beings who were being seen all over England and then, shortly afterwards, the world.

There were behind-the-scenes machinations during that time that I knew nothing about until much later. People have told me that they wanted to ditch me and get an American leading man in, or somebody 'stronger', to work with Diana. Others suggested that they wanted to fire Diana and bring in an American girl. Brian Clemens revealed to me that I was nearly fired on two occasions. I've no idea when this happened, but it might have been when Diana proved such a major success in the black and white shows. I'd been told earlier that they wanted to ditch me and team Honor Blackman with another man! I don't know if any of these things are true, but I do know that we, the prin-

cipal actors, were always kept in the dark, until *they* wanted us to donate our services for some publicity stunt or another.

A glaring example of the presumptuousness of ABPC was the time when their representatives came to us and said, "You're going to Germany on the night plane."

We were stunned.

"Why haven't you warned us?" we asked.

"Oh, it's only just come up, during a meeting. There are a thousand people waiting at the airport for you!"

"That's fine," Di told them. "But why do we have to suddenly go *now*, with no prior notice, while we are still filming?"

"Er... well, it's done. You'll have to go!"

That's when Di turned and showed her true mettle and said, "*I'm* not going. How *dare* you come in and tell me that we're to go to Germany, within a day."

They mumbled something about this being decided in conference.

I very rarely lose my temper, and I didn't do so on this occasion. I was nevertheless force-

Laurie Johnson

Laurie Johnson's music for *The Avengers* is still fondly remembered. Here, he recalls his involvement with the series:

In 1964 the very experienced and successful film producer Julian Wintle took over the making of *The Avengers*. The intention was to make the series on film, in the hope that this would enable *The Avengers* to be sold outside the UK. Julian invited me to join him as composer. We had worked together before on feature films, including *Tiger Bay*, and got on very well. It was intended to make each episode as one would a cinema film. This would mean, for my part, that a separate music score would have to be composed and recorded for each one. I wasn't convinced that within the restrictions of a television timetable we could attain and maintain the standard and quality we aimed at in feature films. But Julian was very persuasive and I agreed.

He was also wise enough to know that Albert Fennell was the man to put at the helm. Albert's vast experience in films —*Tunes of Glory*, *This Sporting Life*, *The Horse's Mouth*, etc — was invaluable. He had a very rare blend of creative sensitivity and an ability to organise and galvanise in his own quiet, charming and courteous way. We all had to learn to accelerate the creative and practical aspects of our crafts, hopefully without lowering standards.

Albert's guiding hand was, I am certain, the one supreme factor which made *The Avengers* films the success they were and still are. This is not, in any way, to underestimate the contribution of Patrick Macnee's and Diana Rigg's beautifully timed performances of real quality (and later on, Linda Thorson), or Brian Clemens' very individual talent for combining style, wit and so many ingenious plots; or the rest of us.

When *The Avengers* made the unprecedented achievement, for a British-made show, of being on a major American network and attracting big audiences coast to coast, the consequences for the schedule were considerable. We had to work to the delivery requirements of the network. I'm still not quite sure how we all made it! For my part, it meant that on a Monday, for instance, Albert and I would run a fine cut of an episode and decide what sequences needed music. Then I would go away and compose sometimes up to forty minutes of music, and record it the following Monday — something that one would normally take four weeks over in feature films.

In all, I composed around fifty hours of music for the series. And in spite of the pressure over three years or more, I enjoyed it, mainly due to Albert and Brian's professionalism and sense of fun.

Later, the three of us took over the copyright of *The Avengers* and made *The New Avengers* series with our own company. I think that our choice of Joanna Lumley and Gareth Hunt proved to be inspired. When the time came that we felt we had no intentions of ever wanting to make any more *Avengers*, we let the rights relapse. We went on to make *The Professionals* series.

Albert and I remained partners when we took over Gainsborough Pictures, with ex-*Avengers* director John Hough, to make films of Dame Barbara Cartland's romantic novels. Tragically Albert died after the making of the first film, and John and I completed three others. Albert is sadly missed, but *The Avengers* films stand as a memorial to his talent and dogged attention to detail and quality. ■

ful. I turned to them and told them in no uncertain terms that Diana and I would *not* be going at such short notice.

We didn't go, but Di and I did visit Germany several weeks later and also spent a delightful, all expenses paid weekend in Paris before returning to the studio.

That was the first sign of real solidarity and I think it was then that Diana really came to love me. She realised she had an ally. Before that she had been fighting these battles by herself. Thereafter, whenever 'they' wished to discuss something with us, they fell in with our request to choose a time when we were not working. They might even invite us out to lunch. Actually, they never did that, but we had stopped them from suddenly turning up at our dressing rooms screaming, "Diana! Pat! Will you..."

Many familiar faces had disappeared from the production team. I never understood why.

Roger Marshall provides a feasible solution:

'I worked on eight film episodes, with no less than six different directors. So much for continuity of style. It was like Tigger's favourite breakfast, as each fresh director arrived at the coalface. John Krish, Gerry O'Hara, Don Leaver, Charles Crichton, Peter Duffell... each in turn was heralded as 'the definitive *Avengers* director'. Each seemed to complete an episode and then vanish. It was my contention (and still is) that the definitive directors were left behind. A production meeting, hosted by Julian and Albert, still lingers in the mind. Armed with his first *Avengers* script, the new director kicked off with three incredibly banal suggestions. Conversation stopped and eyes were lifted to the ceiling. Eventually the director broke the uneasy silence. "Sorry, chaps. Drop too much whisky last night." A CV full of credits on *The Saint* and *The Baron* wasn't the best recommendation for working on *The Avengers*.'

By this time the show was number one in the ratings and Di Rigg and I had got to be very full of ourselves. We were about to be brought down to earth with a bump. Director Sidney Hayers was working with us at the time.

We came onto the set and started to amble our way through the scene. Find the body and the clues, say the lines... Suddenly Sidney stopped us cold.

"Diana. Patrick," he said. "Is this the way you usually do it?"

"Yes," I replied. "This *is* the way we usually do it because it's usually like this." (Sid knew that, of course. He'd directed several of the black and white shows. It was simply his way of jolting us back to reality.)

He said, "Well, not with me it isn't, because

it's so *bad*! Let's start to rethink this scene. There's a lot more here than you're putting in to it."

We looked at him in stunned silence, but he'd grabbed our attention.

"Now, look," he continued. "Don't be so full of yourselves." Well, he didn't say precisely that, but he meant it. "Let's try this scene again and make it as vibrant and interesting as we can."

We explained that it was only a *television* series. The look on his face said it all.

"It's no use at all looking at it like that," he said. "You're number one, sure, but you've got to *earn* it!"

Diana and I were pretty impressed by this.

As director **Robert Day** recalls, forces beyond our control sometimes put paid to the best laid schemes:

'I remember how we would sit around on the set during shooting time rewriting the script and Albert Fennell would appear and be furious! I don't think I ever finished a show in the allocated ten days! And ten days was an absolute luxury compared to the six or seven days we were allowed in Hollywood. But conditions were so different shooting in Elstree.

'I remember rehearsing a scene with Diana and Patrick. I'd just got the scene right and it was 5.45pm. We had just shot the first take and suddenly all the lights went out. A voice with a very strong Scots accent declared that he was the shop steward: it was time to go home. I pleaded with him, stating that I only needed another ten minutes, but I never got it and we had to shoot the scene the following morning. I was so angry. I went storming up to the front office and took it out on Jimmy Wallis the studio manager. I then went to my car to go home. Still seething, I tore away from the curb, misjudged my distance, and ripped off the rear fender on a fire hydrant! That was not my day!

'I also remember often having to wait for the various electronic devices we used to work properly before we could continue.'

The time came when Diana's current contract was due to expire, and she made a final decision to leave the show!

I felt wretched, but once again, because of my own psyche, my lack of courage, I didn't say anything. I was too wound up in my own personal heartache. Kate had entered my life again. The neurosurgeon had walked out on her, she was left alone, so I welcomed her back. Why, I'll never know.

What I should have done with Diana was say to her, "Look. You're having a bad time. I'm having a bad time. Let's get together and

Above: The show was number one in the ratings and we were on top of the world.

Left: Director James Hill explains how he wants Diana to react to her 'Epic' encounter.

make this thing work. Let's make it so successful that we'll forget about the bad times." I *didn't*! I stupidly said, "Well, if you feel like that, of course you must go." Can you imagine?! Sometime later, she said to me, "Pat. If only you had been stronger with me, more forceful, and said, 'No! You've got to stay!' and forgotten your own troubles with your damn stupid wife, we would have gone on and done another two years together... and it would have been great!"

I didn't, because I hadn't the courage... that's all it really needed, guts. One has a sort of instinctive courage, but it's not reflective or analytical. I can't face up to things. I couldn't then and I can't now, although I'm much better at decision taking. I've always found it difficult to face reality, but easy to face going onto a set. I can hide there, you see, lose myself in the character.

Conscious of the worsening situation that had been building up between Diana and the people at ABPC, I should have stepped in earlier and said my piece, no matter what the cost. Throughout the whole of my time with *The Avengers*, I never did... well, not in any major way. I'd complain about this, groan about that, but I never, ever went out on a limb for any of my partners, or anyone else for that matter. My equanimity was extraordinary — the exterior equanimity. Underneath I was full of hidden resentment, turmoil and incipient migraine. But outwardly, I was this cool man. A man who used to brace himself in the mornings to meet Diana and *know* that she would be in a bad mood, but a man who was totally unable to say, "Listen, darling. Let's sit down and talk."

It must have been very, very bad for her, but I said *nothing*.

So once again, it was no thanks to me that Diana forged her way through the dilatory waffle of the people at ABPC — and the guilt just sits on one.

What perturbed her most, I suspect, was that the work seemed to be going on forever. We were now so close to the ABC delivery dates that we were working a fourteen hour day on two, sometimes three episodes simultaneously! When she'd asked them to sit down with her and work out ways and means of completing the production, their reply was to threaten her with an eight-week extension clause in her contract! Tired and anxious to be done with the series, she thought that they were running away from her criticism and justifiable concern. How she overcame this and agreed to do another twelve shows, only Diana knows.

What neither of us knew — *none* of us, including Albert Fennell and Brian Clemens — was that while Diana and her agent were

grappling with the terms and conditions of her new contract, an executive at ABPC had suggested to the company that they should make it a priority to look for a suitable replacement for Diana as soon as possible. Neither did we know that make-up, physical and speaking tests with several actresses had *already* been filmed.

With hindsight, the executive was morally correct to set in motion contingency plans before the ink was dry on Diana's contract. ABPC's deadline with ABC in America made it a matter of urgency that they either confirmed Diana was staying with the show, or sell strongly the new girl they proposed to use. So, while it cannot be argued that Diana was perceived by everyone, including myself, as being an essential — perhaps irreplaceable — element of the successful formula, one had to keep in mind the showbiz maxim, "The show must go on." And it did, but the work was vexatious and unwonted at first.

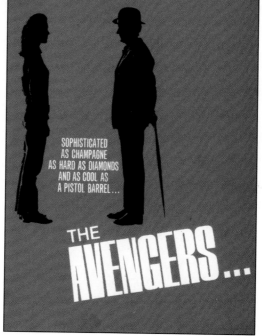

SOPHISTICATED AS CHAMPAGNE AS HARD AS DIAMONDS AND AS COOL AS A PISTOL BARREL...

THE AVENGERS...

Left: The cover of a brochure promoting the first colour series.

Opposite above: On location for a publicity shoot, circa September 1966.

Opposite below: Mrs Peel can't believe her eyes. There's a man on the ceiling playing 'The Winged Avenger'.

After her final *Avengers* episode, I kept in touch with Diana but didn't see her again until 1973, when she was approached to play in a television series, as a female sheriff in a Western town. Unfortunately, Leonard Stern, who had done so many great shows, changed his mind and decided to just have her working in a store. This made her a passive character, which is the direct opposite to what she is. Di is an 'out there' person, dominant, someone in front. So the show did not work for her, despite being directed by the world's greatest television comedy director, Jay Sandrich, who worked on *The Cosby Show*, *The Mary Tyler Moore Show* and, way back, dozens of other wonderful programmes.

I was working in *Sleuth* on Broadway at the time. Diana came to see me and asked, "Will you please come on my show, Pat?" I said that I would. When I finished *Sleuth* and was back in California, Di's American agent phoned me and said, "You are going to do the *Diana* show, Pat."

"How much are you paying?" I asked.

He said, "Oh, we pay very little, but it's a privilege to do it. It's directed by Jay Sandrich, produced by Leonard Stern and it's on CBS... you know, the *Mary Tyler Moore Show* people."

"My God," I thought, and agreed to be in it. The script was very funny.

Knowing how bad I was at lines, Diana and I rehearsed the episode for a week. We filmed the show live in front of an audience and, although I say it myself, it really was awfully good.

Diana played a character called Diana Smythe, a beautiful young divorcée who worked as a fashion illustrator at Buckley's Department Store in Manhattan. I played a character named Bryan Harris, a celebrated concert pianist with an ego as big as Statten Island!

It was no surprise to find that the script was full of ambiguous references to our previous partnership as Steed and Emma Peel. For instance, in the opening sequence Diana is handed a window display card bearing the message: 'Diana Smythe — you're needed!'

"How on earth did he find me?" asks Di.

What does she mean? *Who* needs her?

"It means the ghost of London past has come back to haunt me," she tells her colleagues, as several people are seen walking about the store carrying placards bearing the same message.

We meet a few minutes later, when Di enters her office and finds me waiting for her, my head in a newspaper, my feet resting on her desk.

"You're late!" I tell her.

"*I'm* late?" she replies.

"You're nine years, seventeen minutes..." I glance at my wristwatch, "...and thirty-two seconds late!"

"I do apologise," says Di.

"You're forgiven."

"How are you?" she asks.

"*I'm* a delight — and you?"

"Charming as ever. However did you find me?"

"When you left, I put salt on your tail. You're not exactly inconspicuous. I went to London Airport and said, 'Where did the tall girl go?' They, recognising my impeccable taste, pointed due West."

And the pay-off...

"Do you know, I often wish I hadn't been such an idiot and walked out on you," I tell her.

"*I* walked out on *you!*" says Di.

Delicious!

At the time, the programme was facing difficulties. Ratings were low, the odds against cancellation high. Indeed, Leonard Stern had let it be known that I was being brought into "capitalise mischievously" on my former *Avengers* relationship with Di, as "a new romantic involvement."

Too late. The show was cancelled a few weeks later. ∎

e completed production of *The Avengers'* fifth season on 22 September 1967, nine days over schedule and without Diana, who had left us a week earlier to rejoin the Royal Shakespeare Company.

Then, suddenly, I was back in the studio again doing tests with the actresses who had been shortlisted as Diana's replacement. I don't know how many girls they tested, but I then did a short character sketch with three or four of them. Linda — who, it has to be said, I thought was too young to partner me (I was forty-five at the time) — Jane Merrow, Tracey Reed and Mary Peach.

The tests were shipped to America and seen by a distinguished panel of ABC executives. Their decision was unanimous. No contest — Linda was my new partner.

Not long afterwards, Howard Thomas called me into his office at Hanover Square. Citing the episode called 'The Superlative Seven' as an example, he said, "Patrick, Steed is getting so weak that Diana Rigg is rescuing *you*. Donald Sutherland moves in to threaten you — and you just duck! That's not the way it's supposed to be, Pat."

"What do you mean?" I said by way of retort. "In that one, Diana just happens to be there, having been away on holiday for the best part of the episode. She comes in and rescues me. What's wrong with that? It seems to be quite a good balance. In 'The House That Jack Built', she was alone for almost the entire story and *I* came in and rescued *her*. It's a balance."

"No," he said. "It makes you look so weak; so unmasculine. We've got to change that. We're firing Fennell and Clemens!"

"What!?" I said, thunderstruck that anyone could contemplate such a thing.

"We've got John Bryce coming in. He's taking over the show. He'll breathe new life into it, inject more reality into the plots."

I was devastated. But it happened!

The fact that ABPC had obviously been discussing ways of taking the show away from Brian and Albert was an incredibly ironic situation when you look at it straight on.

During the second season of Diana Rigg shows, we'd been nominated for *two* Emmy awards. Brian and Albert were the architects of those nominations and so to fire them — to even *consider* getting rid of them — was unbelievable!

I was never told why they were booted off the show. It was alleged that Bryce had suggested to ABPC that Brian Clemens had allowed my character to become weak and absurd. I don't know if the story about Bryce is true, but someone set the wheels in motion. Albert and Brian disappeared from the scene.

A couple of weeks later, we started filming the first episode of the new season.

———

Those first few weeks with John Bryce were...

Linda makes her début in the British newspapers.

FORGET-ME-KNOT

At the press junket to launch Linda as my new partner.

strange! There was Linda and me, a director named Robert Asher and John, who seemed totally out of his depth and couldn't even complete the first two or three episodes! When John Bryce worked with Richard Bates on the Blackman shows, he was a deeply sweet man, very supportive and an excellent producer. Now, he was a disaster! I've never understood why. People tell me it's because he had cut his teeth in the videotaped television environment, which apparently required no understanding of the *visual* grammar, lighting and editing techniques used in *film*-making. I don't know, but Bryce was certainly in way over his head.

The first day of shooting at a location in Radlett, Hertfordshire, was a prophecy of what lay ahead. Plans to film with the Bentley were forestalled when Bryce failed to check if the vehicle had been hired. It hadn't. We lost several hours filming. By the fourth day of shooting we had little more than a couple of minutes of usable film in the can and Bryce was forced to call in the second unit to work alongside the main team, with the consequent effect on costs. As producer, Bryce was the man ultimately responsible for keeping the show on schedule and it was obvious that he lacked the requisite experience. Things got progressively worse.

Time and again I tried to maintain the standard of what we'd achieved before, but whenever I suggested something, Bryce would cut me down.

"No!" he'd roar. "That won't work. No, Patrick. No, no, no! Do it *my* way."

The trouble was, his way was wrong! I stopped trying after a time and did what I've always done in times of crisis. I did nothing! The show slipped further and further behind schedule.

Don Sharp was hired to direct the second show. His memories of those laborious times are comparable to mine:

'While shooting *The Champions* at ATC Elstree, I ran into Gordon Scott, who asked if I would be interested in directing more television episodes — a new series of *The Avengers* was in the pipeline. I had seen and admired quite a lot of the earlier series and had also been friendly with Albert Fennell in my days with Independent Artists at Beaconsfield. I was amazed when Gordon told me that Albert and Brian Clemens were no longer connected with the series, which was being given a new look, but... *The Avengers without* Albert and Brian?

'Within a week, Howard Thomas and John Bryce had said yes to me joining the team. I would join *The Avengers* in October. Howard and I had worked together for several years at the Pathé documentary unit, but John Bryce was new to me. According to Gordon Scott, he was "said to be a whiz-kid." Thomas was full of praise for John Bryce and expected great things from him... just the man to give the show a new image, a new look, and take it to a wider audience.

'I met John Bryce at Elstree, after I had read the first draft of Terry Nation's 'Invasion of the Earthmen', which was a well-constructed action-adventure piece with a good balance of location and exterior. But it didn't have the personality of *The Avengers*. If this was to be the start of a new partnership — Steed and Tara — then some serious thinking was need-ed. Patrick and Diana had been a *team* — two experienced actors of equal stature with strong individual personalities. Linda Thorson had been cast to replace Diana. Much younger than Patrick, and far less experienced than Diana, her personality was quite different. (In today's jargon, it was re-active rather than pro-active.) Repeating the old relationship was not fair to her. She was being asked to step into Diana's shoes: she should have been given new shoes of her own. The whole basis of the relationship, I believed, needed to be radically different. I tried to talk to John Bryce about it, but each time he would go off at a tangent about how *different* the show was going to look. To be blunt, he seemed more concerned with finding an alternative to Diana Rigg's leather gear than with matters of character and relationship, and was difficult to pin down for discussions on *any* aspect of making the show. This he left to others.

'I finally made the decision to give up my attempt to establish a new Steed-Tara relation-ship. I was concerned, too, about voicing any worries that might feed back to Linda. She was friendly, likeable, wanted to make a success of the part and was prepared to work at it, but her confidence was not, I felt, sufficiently strong to deal with any doubts on my part. By that I don't mean that she lacked confidence in her own abilities. I felt she was... well, bewildered. She was constantly being rushed off to photo calls, publicity, costume fittings and the like — all important, all necessary — but the very core of her work as an actress, her character and relationship to Steed, seemed to have no place in the new scheme of things. Patrick was splen-did. Calm, helpful and supportive.'

During those first few weeks, Linda was hav-ing a ball. I was hating every minute of it.

"What am I doing here?" I thought.

I didn't want to be there. It was humiliating, it was tough and I wished I'd left the show. Ian Hendry used to tell me that the series should have more dimensions than appeared in the script — a conviction I held onto throughout

Above: The start of a new partnership. A scene from the unfinished episode 'The Great Great Britain Crime'.

the whole of the Honor Blackman time, and was revived again with Diana Rigg — but now the enthusiasm had slipped away.

Despite Hugh Cruttwell, then head of RADA, telling me, "You're getting our top student, Pat. She's the best," I couldn't help thinking that Linda should never have been given the role. The fact that she left RADA with an Honours Diploma and a prize for the best student in voice production should have told me something, but it didn't. That she had no experience whatsoever of working in front of the camera did, and I really never gave Linda the chance to prove herself. Not until Ray Austin laid it on the line.

"Pat," he said, "I know you think Linda is not the right one for us, but they like her and want to keep her in." ('They' being the ABC network executives.)

"They're wrong, Ray. I honestly don't think that we should," I told him.

"Give her a chance, Pat." Ray said. " *Make* it work — take her under your wing."

There was no arguing with that, and everyone else on the team did seem to get along well with Linda. Was I missing something?

John Bryce, meanwhile, was sending the show down the tubes. He ranted and raved and continued to dismiss every suggestion I made with a venomous tirade. I *knew* that the show was crumbling, but I said, and did, nothing. I just went along with it. I went home, I drank and felt utterly miserable.

Six weeks later Bryce was fired and Brian and Albert mysteriously returned.

———

Many reasons have been advanced as to why they were reinstated — most of it conjecture. I suggest it was dictated by good old-fashioned common sense. Realising that John Bryce was in danger of grinding the show into obscurity, ABPC (now merged with Thames Television) had no alternative but to eat humble pie and bring back Albert and Brian. A class act, they *knew* what made the show tick.

The news that Albert and Brian were taking control again — this time as full-blown producers — gave a boost to everyone's morale.

As **Don Sharp** confirms, things changed for the better overnight:

'During the production of 'A Murderous Connection', John Bryce's name was deleted from the casting advice notes and Brian Clemens' name was added to the distribution list. A revised screenplay ('The Curious Case of the Countless Clues') was issued on 6 December, two days after the original start date.

'For several weeks we had fog, rain, snow — delays which took us across the Christmas break. On 27 December pink pages (ie re-

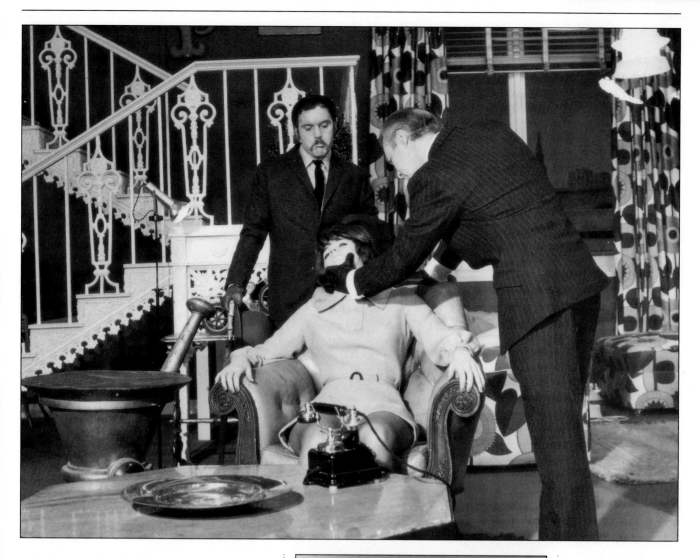

writes) were issued. These were not merely alterations to scenes that hadn't yet been shot, but sequences already filmed and now rewritten. The 'feel' began to change. We were back in the special world of *The Avengers*: little contact with the 'normal' world, a minimum number of characters, one special protagonist for Steed, and Steed and Tara working as *equals*, each with positive action. Her character was no longer the rookie, the script had her contributing equally, in an individual manner, to the action. Linda was certainly happier now, more confident, enjoying each day on the studio floor. But then everyone's morale was higher. There was a strong guiding hand, someone firmly in charge who had the imagination and cared about quality, a man who was the guardian of the singular 'feel' of *The Avengers* — Albert Fennell.'

After viewing rushes of the films produced by John Bryce, Brian wrote 'The Forget-Me-Knot'. Completed in eight days, under the accomplished direction of Jimmy Hill, the tale bid farewell to Mrs Peel and introduced Tara King

Above: Earle and Gardiner rig things in Tara's flat to make it seem that Steed has killed her after a struggle. (From 'The Curious Case of the Countless Clues'.)

The Forget-Me-Knot

In *The Avengers'* only 'crossover' episode, Mrs Peel gets the chance to (briefly) meet her replacement, as she leaves to be reunited with her husband. And if you think Mr Peel looks somewhat familiar... I played him as well!

'The Forget-Me-Knot' (Episode # 131, by Brian Clemens).

INT. STEED'S APARTMENT. DAY.
STEED (INTO PHONE): Yes, Mother... I've seen the papers. Yes, it looks as though I'll be needing a replacement... Well, as soon as possible. You know my taste... I'll trust your judgement.
EMMA ENTERS.
EMMA: Steed! (EXCITED.) You've seen the newspapers?
STEED: Yes.
EMMA: Trust him to make a dramatic reappearance... Found in the jungle...
STEED: The Amazonian jungle.
EMMA: Corny.
STEED: *Ridiculous.*
EMMA: They've flown him back. He'll be picking me up in a few minutes.
STEED: *Here?*
EMMA (CLOSES): Always keep your bowler on in times of stress — and a watchful eye open for diabolical masterminds.
STEED: I'll remember.
EMMA: Goodbye, Steed.
SHE KISSES HIS CHEEK. TURNS, WALKS TO DOOR. STEED WATCHES HER GO.
STEED: *Emma.* (SHE STOPS. TURNS, LOOKS BACK.) Thanks.
EMMA EXITS.

INT. STEED'S APARTMENT. STAIRWAY.
EMMA AND TARA.
TARA: Excuse me, Apartment 3?
EMMA: At the top of the stairs.
TARA: Thanks.
EMMA: Ahem. He likes his tea stirred — anti-clockwise.
TARA MIMICS THE STIRRING MOTION.
EMMA (NODS): Yes.

INT/EXT. STEED'S APARTMENT WINDOW.
STEED AT WINDOW. NO DIALOGUE.

EXT. STEED'S APARTMENT. WINDOW.
EMMA GETS INTO CAR. THEY DRIVE OFF. NO DIALOGUE.

INT/EXT. STEED'S APARTMENT. WINDOW
STEED WATCHES THEM GO. NO DIALOGUE.

EXT. STEED'S APARTMENT. MEWS
LONG SHOT. MEWS. AS CAR GOES AWAY. NO DIALOGUE.

INT. STEED'S APARTMENT.
STEED AT WINDOW. TARA ENTERS. HE TURNS.
TARA: Mother sent me.
STEED: Ra-boom-di-ay...
TARA: Tea?
STEED (*LAUGHS*). ∎

— a nice touch being that Albert and Brian decided to open the show with the Di Rigg title credits and end the show with the Steed/Tara animated and live action credits produced by John Bryce.

My scenes with Di, who had agreed to return to the show briefly so Emma could say goodbye, were shot over a four day period — a heart-rending and difficult time. It's a moment I will never forget, because I was so desperately unhappy that she was leaving. When she finally came up, kissed me on the cheek and said the line, "Always keep your bowler on in times of stress, and a watchful eye open for diabolical masterminds", I cried. I just knew that I was going to miss her so much. She'd been *everything*. Her energy. Her sense of fun. The total throwaway manner in which she'd brush back her hair after she'd just demolished two or three men in one go. Her certainty — everything about her. To paraphrase Rex Harrison, I'd grown accustomed to her face — *and loved it*!

THE
AVENGERS

this inimitable series enters its 4th great year in the major markets of the world

Above: Filming the first title credits.

Left: Another promotional brochure.

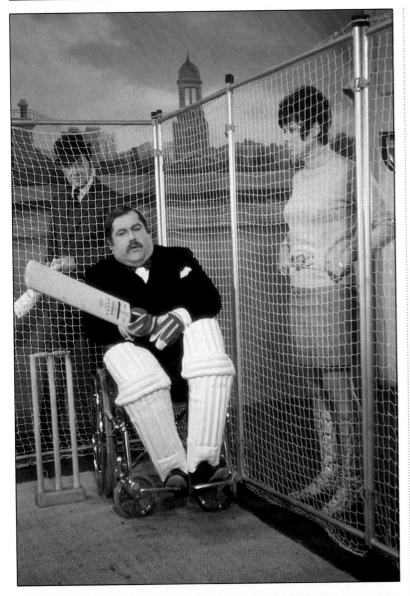

Diana filmed the fleeting hand-over sequence with Linda, and then she was gone for good!

———

One thing I found important in the previous episodes, and something my partners and I did instinctively, was the touch of academicism and quiet authority we brought to the series. There was never anyone above us in the pecking order. Well, perhaps there was during the Hendry and Blackman seasons, with the likes of 'One-Ten', but never in the Di Rigg shows. We didn't have the police sergeant on the desk, or the Detective Super of Scotland Yard, or even the head of MI5 pushing us about. (Quite right too, because now we know how Sir Anthony Blunt got away with it for so long. If you projected a natural air of authority, you got away with all sorts of things, as Blunt did whilst being a traitor. With his breeding and background, nobody questioned him.)

Steed's background was not like the wealth and status of, say, the characters played by Robert Wagner and Stefanie Powers in *Hart to Hart*, which, being an American programme, was stated overtly. Steed's wealth and position was just *accepted*; you didn't have to speak about it. That's very British — you just *were*. So when we suddenly got 'Mother' in the Linda Thorson shows, I thought it became very boring having Steed report to this man, just to be sent off on his mission.

For many of the Honor Blackman episodes, and always during the Di Rigg shows, we were *there* at the scene. It didn't have to be explained *how* we got there, we just *were*. We weren't cute, we weren't clever — we were real, two people who had a lot of common sense. The Bond films are different, of course. Bond has to report back to 'M' and check in with 'Q'. We didn't. Where we came from didn't matter. We arrived. We investigated. We left. Things didn't have be stated or made obvious.

So, this ridiculous business with Mother left me cold. Paddy Newell, I'm bound to say, was a delightful, self-effacing, deeply interesting chap. We grew very fond of each other during those eighteen months, but Mother bored the pants off me.

———

At the beginning of the sixth series, I was starting to have a weight problem which, though it worried me, I pretended wasn't there. I still had a figure that, at a pinch, could be surrounded by a suit. I still had good movement and my mind still responded quickly, by instinct, to changing situations, but my nerve endings had been pushed to the limit by the day-to-day hassle of arguing with John Bryce.

Nevertheless, concerned about appearing

with a twenty year old leading lady, I convinced myself that I had to do something.

Solace came when an eminent Harley Street specialist, who numbered many famous stars among his patients, prescribed a drug for me — Durophet.

He prescribed two Durophet a day. They gave me tremendous energy. I felt marvellous, lost twenty-six pounds and my suits had to be taken in at the seams. Time spent on the set became easier and I started to enjoy myself, but the prescription almost caused my downfall.

What I didn't understand, until I went to Australia after filming *The Avengers* to play *The Secretary Bird* on stage, was that Durophet was one of the most dangerous amphetamines in existence. I couldn't get it on prescription there and to get off it I had to go cold turkey — but I still didn't realise that it was such a dangerous drug. I thought it was reducing my weight, which it did. Since then, I've started to study the effects of speed and what it does to the body. Whether it's given to you by a Harley Street specialist to reduce your weight or bought on the street to give you a high, the result is the same: you do everything at double

time, don't listen to anyone, and are impatient with everything and everybody, particularly your nearest and dearest. It's a devastating thing. The only positive aspect is that it takes off the weight, because you don't want to eat, you don't want to think, you just want to react, and you move around like a jazzed-up puppet. In retrospect, the fact that I gave some to a friend in England, who went down the Great West Road and had to stop halfway because she went *blind* for an hour or so, and had to rest up by the side of the road, should have told me something! The drug was banned shortly afterwards by the British Medical Council.

I learned later that the Harley Street specialist had prescribed Durophet for Linda at the request of ABPC, who considered that she was overweight.

It must be said, however, that although Linda was taking the Durophet, she never behaved the way I did, although the drug did make both of us very chatty.

During the making of the series, I was awfully flamboyant and, according to our PR lady Marie Donaldson, totally impossible to be

THE AVENGERS AND ME

with. What I didn't understand, until she told me, was that I couldn't stop talking: the Durophet made me talk at ninety miles an hour constantly. (Doctors tell me that it's not possible, but I think that I've still got a vestige of it in my system now. I'm certainly liable to take over a conversation. People think it's because I'm an actor and I feel I'm on stage. It isn't really that, it's the residue of the feeling that I had to say everything *then*, otherwise I would forget because I was living at an enormously high speed.)

I also couldn't even relate to my part in the Thorson shows. I couldn't make the character work, or at least I thought so.

As I say, at the beginning I literally wanted Linda to go away. On many occasions, mainly because of my own domestic problems which made me very unhappy for a long time, I was derisive, dismissive and downright rude to her. Most of the directors took a fancy to her — in a professional way — and most, I think, found me a pain in the arse. Indeed, I don't

know how Linda put up with me. I must have been intolerable!

The turnaround in our relationship came a few days into the production of the second Fennell/Clemens episode, 'Split'. Linda told me that she was being subjected to a level of crass behaviour by the people at ABPC, some of whom were treating her with the same disregard they had previously shown Diana Rigg.

They would arrive on set, or call at her dressing room, and say things like, "Linda, we don't like that dress. We don't like that blouse... and try not to wear that coat, will you luv — it makes you look like a rag doll!" That they'd taken to belittling her in front of anybody within earshot sent my juices flowing. They'd never gone quite *that* far with Di Rigg, and I wasn't prepared to allow it to happen now.

I advised Linda that she was not to meet them, attend unsolicited interviews or go anywhere, unless I or someone else escorted her — and she didn't. Things became easier between us after that. Whereas previously I had been unsupportive, I befriended her.

She explained how she wanted to take risks with her character, to make Tara that little bit different from Emma Peel and Cathy Gale, but felt she hadn't been afforded the opportunity to express herself or the incentive to make the transition.

Impressed with her 'gutsy' approach — she proved to have an amazing amount of savvy for a girl just starting out — I championed her cause.

I wanted us to have the same easy, friendly relationship I'd had with my previous partners. We were, after all, going to be spending the best part of our working lives together, so I wanted it to be a happy relationship for both our sakes.

I might have wished for a more accomplished actress, of course, but my concerns about having a screen romance of sorts, even a light-hearted one, with a girl just a few years older than my daughter, soon melted away and I got round to thinking that her youth would perhaps be contagious. Her vitality was already giving a new edge to the partnership.

As our plots became increasingly mad, I felt

With Linda I became more tender towards my partner, tougher on the villains.

that Steed must become more human — a man who liked to *think* his way out of trouble, a man who preferred thought to violence. The relationship he shared with Tara was much lighter than before, so I became more tender towards my partner, tougher on the villains. Brian Clemens latched on to this and the scripts became funnier, more extreme — some say better.

With Linda, a slight element of hero-worship was added. The grateful pecks on the cheek at the conclusion of a hazardous assignment became more prolific, but there was still never any suggestion that Tara and Steed went to bed together. Such thoughts were left to one's mind's eye. Perhaps they did. Maybe they didn't. The viewer had to decide for themselves if, having spent the night at Steed's apartment, Tara's honour was still intact.

In the past, whenever anyone has mentioned the Thorson shows, my thoughts about them lingered on the episodes I had seen. Because of many painful personal memories, during the last twenty years or so I could not, and did not, watch more than a couple of the shows we made together, until Dave Rogers mailed me a compilation video of a dozen or so episodes and asked me to comment on them.

They came as a revelation! Outstandingly good, I realise now that I have grossly maligned Linda for a long time! At the time of making them I used to think that people were saying, "Oh my God, more of *The Avengers*, more of the same," because they'd seen enough of us. I thought we were flogging a dead horse. How wrong I was. Now, many years later, I realise that we weren't. They rate as some of the very best episodes that were ever done.

I understand now why Hugh Cruttwell told me how lucky we were to have her. Indeed we were. With Linda I became much more of a leading man than I ever realised. Free of affectation, I became a *straight* hero, which I'd never been before. I'd been slightly off, slightly subservient to the women. Linda put me almost in the position of being her knight in shining armour, because that's when I became fit, thin and mad. As she told me recently, "You know, Patrick, because I played it as though I loved you, I made you look better." That she most certainly did... except for my sideburns. Whatever possessed me to wear them?

I remember Brian Clemens saying to me, "Do you *really* need those, Pat?"

I didn't, of course. At the time I rather thought that they made me look better, more handsome... more like a film star. I suppose I thought it was the 'in' thing to do. Instead, they made me look like a back street dealer in pornographic magazines. Was I so self-deluded? Was it the effect of taking the Durophet?

Whatever it was, they look ridiculous!

I meet people today, many, many people, who think that the shows I did with Linda are my finest hour and that Linda was the *best* ever *Avengers* girl. Friends in California have all said that she was the best. The French went wild about her. She became one of their favourite stars and appeared on the cover of *Paris Match*. They *still* say that she's the best girl!

During the time we were making the show, Linda was never anything but sweet, darling and encouraging. Since then I've done her a great disservice.

I take this time to apologise to her.

———

Working long hours in the studio left one feeling drained, and never more so than at Elstree. For some unknown reason, the people who ran the studio kept us on Stage 5 throughout our stay. We were occasionally allowed to use the main stages, but not very often.

The trouble was, Stage 5 wasn't soundproof. So every time an aeroplane flew overhead, or two people walked by talking, we had to stop filming, which increased the pressure on the unit and incurred extra cost.

I remember that things got so bad that a facetious studio technician pinned a notice to the studio door: 'NO TALKING around this building while shooting goes on inside!' This failed to silence the birds, who had nested in the ceiling rafters and chirped merrily away on many an afternoon!

Midway through the production of season six, I was given Elizabeth Taylor's dressing room; two wonderful lilac-coloured rooms that she'd had when she was at the studio making *Secret Ceremony* and her husband Richard Burton was up the road making *Where Eagles Dare*. I was told I could have it only if I didn't want it redecorated. I loathe any shade of purple, but lived with that mauve wallpaper for nearly two years!

One of my happiest memories from this time was working with the late Jimmy Jewel on the episode entitled 'Look — (stop me if you've heard this one) But There Were These Two Fellers...', the longest title in the *Avengers* canon and one of the most enjoyable working experiences of my life. Directed beautifully, with a light and deft touch by Jimmy Hill, working on the show was a pure delight.

A master of comedic timing, Jimmy Jewel gave generously of his time and energy to me and we did an extraordinary fight together, one of the best and most hilarious fights filmed for *The Avengers*... indeed, for any show. All that bashing over the head like Punch and Judy is, I suggest, the only way to treat violence. It was a marvellous scene, with the gorgeous craziness of the multiple change of costumes. Jimmy

Above: Those sideburns! Whatever possessed me to wear them?

Left: The fight with Jimmy Jewel in 'Look (stop me...' is, I suggest, the only way to treat violence.

Opposite below: Tara's knight in shining armour.

brought a wonderful, extravagant talent to the show and the fight was so well orchestrated that Jimmy and I said that we were prepared to work extra hours to get it right. It's an episode that I remember with enormous affection and love to show to friends.

Fights in *The Avengers* were always good. In the Thorson shows they became tremendous fun and were always based on comedy — crazy comedy. Needless to say, I just loathed doing most of the fight scenes, but they were always brilliantly thought out. Ray Austin, Joe Dunne, Rocky Taylor and Paul Weston all doubled me at one time or another and made me look so good.

Again, note that very rarely do I use a gun. When I do, it just happens to be there, like in 'Legacy of Death', where I don't start out with a gun, but pick one up from the floor. Or the scene in 'Game', where it is given to me. I'm very proud of that.

Oddly enough, I never acquired any serious personal injury as a result of the action sequences, but my ego was bruised as a result of rescuing the damsel in distress.

Etched in my memory is the day we filmed the scene in 'Love All' where I rescue Tara from the window ledge. For some ridiculous reason, I raced to the window and cracked three or four ribs, yet still managed to pull her back into the room. I was trying to make the scene as realistic as possible. Stupid, really, since Linda's feet were only a few feet from the studio floor!

I didn't realise I was injured at the time. Then, when I went to Australia after the show was finished, someone threw me into a swimming pool and I twisted my back. As a consequence, they discovered the cracked ribs. I ended up in a chiropractor's hands for years afterwards.

———

The sixth season opened in America in March 1968, four months into production (viewers in England had to wait until January 1969 to meet Tara). I remember that we replaced a show called *Custer* in the schedules. People wrote in saying that they didn't mind losing *Custer*, but because of *The Avengers* they'd now never know what happened to him at the battle of the Big Horn! (He lost!)

Viewers warmed to Linda's portrayal of Tara and the show received a favourable response from the critics.

'A problem for the series is the difficulty of keeping it fresh and interesting,' wrote the *Daily Mail*. 'A new heroine every few years does wonders. This episode was concerned mostly with the shooting of people with a drug pellet that produced amnesia, but it did introduce the new girl in Steed's life.

'She is a very pretty, wide-eyed brunette

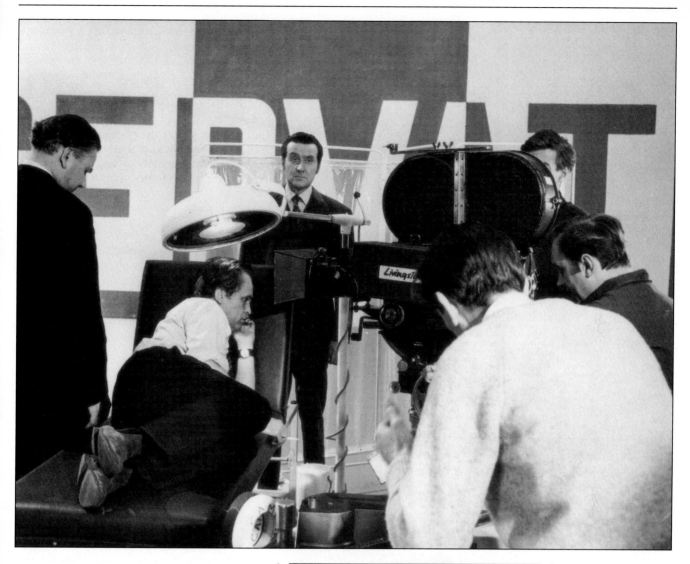

named Linda Thorson and plays an agent named Tara King. She demonstrated at the outset that she is almost as good at hand-to-hand fighting as Mrs Peel. Fans of the series will undoubtedly take the switch over in their stride. The show is remarkable in the way it makes the most vicious evildoing and prolonged slug fests seem part of a sprightly little comedy.'

'Great fun,' thought another, suggesting that Tara lacked Emma's panache, but more than made up for it by her wackiness. 'On this performance, Tara is a sexy tease, a wide-eyed innocent who takes crime-busting in her stride, ably abetted by mentor John Steed.'

'Miss Thorson, who clearly has no desire to wear another woman's shoes, is playing it as an all-girl role. It's a technique for which she is unquestionably well equipped.'

A few months into filming, Linda took a holiday and the producers teamed Steed with a character called Lady Diana Forbes-Blakeney, played by actress Jennifer Croxton. I spent a delightful two weeks in her company filming the episode 'Killer', a story about agents dying

Opposite above: The original idea was to make Tara a more feminine heroine. Linda was soon laying the villains out in her own inimitable style.

Opposite below: In a relaxed mood on the set of 'Love All'.

*Above: 'Bizarre'.
Steed and Tara blast
off into outer space.*

*Right: Tara falls
victim to the insid-
ious Interrogators.*

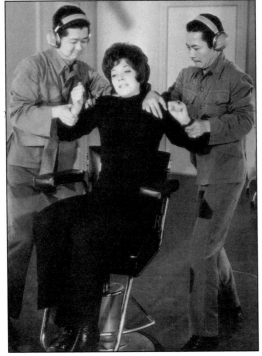

*Opposite above: At
Elstree during the
filming of the
French champagne
commercial.*

*Opposite below:
Working solo Tara
discovers that
it's 'All Done
With Mirrors'.*

by crushing, garrotting, stabbing, electro-cution, rifle bullets, strangulation and poison darts — have I left anything out? — adminis-tered by a computer.

But by then we knew that the writing was on the wall. The ABC network ran the show against *I Dream of Jeannie* and the first half-hour of Rowan and Martin's *Laugh-In* on NBC.

The fact that we were finally clobbered by *Laugh-In* returned to my memory only a few days ago, when I was invited by George Schlat-ter and Roseanne Barr to an evening for Jennifer Saunders and Joanna Lumley. Schlat-ter was the originator and producer of *Laugh-In*, at the time the most popular show on the networks. The odds were stacked against us. Our ratings tumbled and ABC decided to call it a day: they did not wish to continue with another series.

Brian Clemens chose to end the show with the two of us marooned on a rocket — a stroke of genius. An irretrievable situation? Perhaps. But then Steed and his partners had faced such outrageous situations before and *always* emerged with honours.

"Can you get us down?"

"Eventually, yes."

"Eventually?"

"There's no hurry... is there?"

To crib from Brian: "What goes up, must come down."

The critics didn't seem to care one way or the other.

'Its subtlety and high sense of humour has long since been ironed out in the quest for dollars," offered the *Daily Express* arts correspondent. '*The Avengers* is weary and travel-worn,' thought *The Sun*. 'Its gravity has gone. It no longer pulls me. Where is the outrageous invention? The elegant send-up of espionage and sex? Maybe the show hasn't changed and that's the trouble. For we have.'

Perhaps they were right, but we'd had a very healthy run for our money. When Linda and I went up in that rocket, I fully expected that was the last I'd ever see of the show. Little did I know that through Linda I would get back into the ring again with *The New Avengers*. A French champagne commercial I made with her at Elstree was the precursor of producer Rudolph Roffi's decision to revive the show. To this day I can't understand why Linda and I didn't do the new show together, as Roffi considered us a fine twosome. Having the two of us together would have brought *The Avengers* full circle.

Until Linda mentioned it recently, when we were attending the first ever *Television Film Festiff* in Nice together, I'd never thought about the bond of circumstance that ties the show to the beautiful city of Toronto in Canada. Created by Toronto-born Sydney Newman, *The Avengers* was co-produced by Leonard White — not a native Canadian, I grant you, but a man who spent his formative years in the industry in Toronto — and nine years later I bowed out with Toronto-born Linda Thorson!

Had any of us thought about it at the time, we might have made capital of this by, say, opening *The Avengers* up to encompass an international playground. Brian Clemens was always saying that one day Steed and his partner would go abroad occasionally, "although no farther than Europe." We might even have let Linda play Tara in her native tongue! It wouldn't have mattered, and think of the publicity it would have generated!

Toronto would figure once more in the saga, but that was some way down the road.

———

We had a get-together at the end of production. The whole crew attended, including the cast who worked on the last show. I was presented with a watch by Howard Thomas. I

remember that Brian Clemens commented later, "After nine years, *that's* all they can give you, Pat?!"

I was able to make a few remarks, which reflected the warmth that one felt for the crew one had worked with for so long. I made my speech, thanked Howard Thomas for the watch, expressed my sincere thanks to everybody, and mentioned something or other about working on Stage 5, which we were always put on in case feature films came in and they would need the space. What I didn't mention, of course, was *The Avengers* had kept the studio open throughout that time, when they hardly had any features at all apart from the Elizabeth Taylor film *Secret Ceremony* and a couple of Bette Davis shockers. Apart from those, we had been personally responsible for keeping the studio open — by we, I mean *The Avengers*, Roger Moore's *The Saint*, and the ITC shows *The Champions* and *Department S*.

Oddly enough, when I finished the speech I had a tear in my eye!

———

I was reunited with some of the *Avengers* team later in 1969, when I made the film *Mister Jerico*, which was produced by Julian Wintle, directed by Sidney Hayers, written by Philip Levene and had soundtrack music by Laurie Johnson. It had originally been offered to Robert Wagner. Robert Wagner wasn't available, so they got me — again overweight and not really ready to do it.

Mister Jerico was shot on location in Malta, and Connie Stevens, my leading lady, and I stayed at the Dragonara Hotel, a beautiful place next to the beach. On the second day, as I was sitting outside the hotel, Frankie Howerd appeared. He had nothing on but a bathing suit and a toupee. We greeted each other warmly and swam out to a raft, which was moored about 200 yards from the shore. Frankie reached the raft first. The toupee went up and he went down!

We sat there treading water and he was telling me what it was like in Australia, which I was about to visit with *The Secretary Bird*. As ever, Frankie was extremely funny and delightful company.

He said, "Come to dinner with your cast. How many are you?"

"Three or four of us and the director Sid Hayers," I replied.

"Come to my house on Thursday and we'll have dinner," he said.

We turned up at the appointed time, to be met by his companion, who told us, "I'm afraid Frankie's not going to be with you this evening — he's on the roof."

"Why's he on the roof?" I asked, concerned for Frankie's welfare.

"Oh," he said. "When things are bad and it's a full moon, he goes up onto the roof and bays like a dog."

"Oh, really?!" I went up on the roof and there was Frankie, literally baying like a wolf! We didn't get dinner and so we went back to the hotel. I never did find out if he was playing a practical joke on us!

I was reminded of the film years later, when I was making *The New Avengers* at Pinewood. Richard Burton was working at the studio and was given a dressing room just along the corridor from mine. He spotted me one day and called me over.

"Patrick," said Richard. "I saw you in a film the other day, *Mister Jerico*."

"Yes?" I said.

"You know, you could have been a movie star!" he told me.

Alas, this was not a view shared by *Mister Jerico*'s producer, Michael Eisner, who'd said to me when we started filming, "You're too fat. You're too old. I don't like you in the part but, God, as you're in it we'd better go ahead!"

A short while later, when I was in Australia, Thames Television contacted me. They were

*Opposite below:
A KNOckout!*

doing Honor Blackman's *This is Your Life* and asked if I would make a guest appearance. I said yes. We arranged that I would fly in from Los Angeles and they booked me a first class ticket.

I left Australia a few weeks later. After performing the play for three months, I wanted to return to California because I hoped to get back into US television, which I did. I got quite a big part on the NBC show *The Virginian*, in an episode called 'King's Ransom' with James Drury, Lee J. Cobb and Doug McClure.

However, for four months in 1969 I found myself in the midst of the Poseidon Tin Mine stock offer. Shares had been offered at eighty cents and friends were urging me to buy.

"Oooh," I said, "I really can't buy $2,000 worth of shares..."

If I had followed their advice and bought them, and then sold them off when the share price rose to between $125-180, I would have made myself $300,000! But I didn't.

Then I heard from John Mather, the man who later put on the stage version of *The Avengers*,

PATRICK MACNEE · HERBERT LOM
CONNIE STEVENS · MARTY ALLEN
MISTER JERICO
In Colour

and lost his shirt by doing so. He phoned to ask if I was still going to Honor's *This is Your Life*. I told him I wasn't sure. "I've got a part in a TV movie at NBC. I've got to do it."

Still reeling from my foolhardiness with the Poseidon affair, I didn't go! The show went ahead without me... that is to say, I didn't attend in person. They put a call through to me. The line went down and I never got it. They rang again, an hour before the programme was due to begin and I managed to relay a message to Honor over a very bad line.

"Honor, darling. I'm speaking to you from a very long way away in California, and I want to say how very sorry I am that I'm not with you and Maurice.

"This is the fourth year that we would have spent Christmas together, so I want to wish you all — and the children — the very, very best. A big kiss to you all and lots of love."

I believe Honor said, "Oh, we'll miss him this Christmas."

So the truth is that on this occasion I let down Honor out of sheer greed, necessity and desperation for money! I returned to Australia the following year and stayed for eight months.

Honor was the subject of *This is Your Life* again in 1993, this time for BBC TV, in a show presented by Michael Aspel.

Again unable to be there in person, I appeared on film from Palm Springs. "Hello, Honor," I began. "Thirty years ago we started all this and now they're showing it on Channel Four... and what about 'Kinky Boots'! I couldn't believe that. I hoped they'd put it away and no one would listen to it, then suddenly it's top of the pops in the nineties!"

Leonard White put in an appearance, as did Jackie Pallo, the stuntman who Honor had so memorably knocked out. Comedian Ronnie Corbett explained that he couldn't remember the first time they had met.

"If my memory serves me correctly," said Ronnie, "it was when I originally auditioned for the part of Steed. I guess I wasn't quite up to it!" He was joking, I think! ■

Above: Con-man Dudley Jerico sets out to steal the Gemini diamond from corrupt millionaire Victor Rosso.

Opposite above: Face to face. But is Steed Steed?

It was an extraordinary feeling, back in 1975, setting off from America after six years away from England.

I'd left in a hurry in 1969, because my manager said that I had to get out of England as soon as possible. He said that I owed the Inland Revenue £49,000 and warned they could put me in prison.

I was on amphetamines at the time and wasn't in touch with reality at all. So I went to Malibu, walked along the beach, drank whisky and felt completely alone and desperately miserable. I'd been doing nine years of hectic work in which I'd been totally involved... and, of course, had underrated myself. I'd played myself down to such an extent that I thought the series was a complete flop. It wasn't a complete flop. It was just the end of *The Avengers*. Then it turned out that I didn't owe the tax man £49,000 after all...

But before returning to England, and during the same year I made the French champagne commercial which reunited me with Linda Thorson, I took Diana Rigg to 'The Straw Hat Awards'. The awards ceremony was presented by Cary Grant, who read out my résumé. There was mention of Olivier's *Hamlet*, David Niven's *The Elusive Pimpernel* (aka *The Fighting Pimpernel*) and a few other major movies in which I'd served as an extra — or near extra! Grant was an immensely charming man, but hadn't told me that he was going to do this. He read out this list, then introduced me as though I was the co-star! It was desperately embarrassing. Fortunately, I managed to use my wits and make a response speech which was quite amusing. Di said afterwards, "You know, Pat, it's incredible. When our backs are against the wall, we Brits can always come up with something. As I've said, Pat, you're always good on the brink of disaster — and funny with it."

I was playing in *Sleuth* at the time, at the St Charles Dinner Theatre, Illinois, a role I had played for two years on Broadway. After that, I left for England, to play the whole summer in Andrew Sachs' *Made in Heaven*, which eventually was retitled 'Made in Hell', because it was a terrible flop. (The fact that I played five different parts may have had something to do with it!) At the same time, I had to race up to Elstree to film the commercial with Linda, then race back to Chichester again to catch the curtain call.

The commercial was made by Rudolph Roffi. The biggest producer of commercials for French cinemas, Roffi had approached Albert Fennell and Brian Clemens about producing an ad for Laurent Perrier champagne, using Linda and myself as Tara and Steed. It was easier to film the commercial in England than in France, so Albert and Brian contacted some of the old production team and Linda and I filmed the commercial at Elstree. She then returned to Toronto to work in theatre and

At Malibu Beach in California.

TWO BECOME THREE

Above: Filming the Laurent Perrier champagne commercial.

Right: At Chichester with Patricia Routledge in Andrew Sachs' Made in Heaven.

Opposite: Shots from Joanna and Gareth's screen test for the roles of Purdey and Gambit.

television, and I flew off to New York to begin rehearsals for the touring production of *Absurd Person Singular*.

Some very eminent people had played my part in this particular play. When we opened in Toronto, the notice read, 'Macnee best of an *absurdly* inept lot!' In fact, Eric Thompson, a very fine director whose work includes almost all of Alan Ayckbourn's plays (he was also, of course, the father of Emma Thompson), came to Chicago to try and make us a little less inept. At the end, he told me, "Honestly, Pat. I just don't think there's too much I can do!" and he was gone. He was right and we failed in Detroit. Sadly, Eric died far, far too young for such a brilliant and amusing man.

During this run, my agent John Redway rang to say, "They want you for the remake of *The Avengers*."

I was stunned. *What* remake of *The Avengers*? "Who's doing it?" I asked.

"Your old pals Fennell, Clemens and Laurie Johnson."

I thought he was pulling my leg. Brian Clemens had visited me when I was playing *Made in Heaven*, at Chichester, and we met again when filming the champagne commercial, but he'd never said anything then about doing a new series of *The Avengers*. It seems he knew nothing about it at that time. Roffi had asked me if I would *like* to do the series again. "I certainly can't do it in French," I told him and forgot all about it. Roffi obviously hadn't. Several weeks later he contacted Brian and Albert again. "I've got the money. When can we start?" he asked.

———

"It's an awfully good contract," John Redway told me. "You'll be getting £2,000 a week and five per cent of the profits." I never thought to ask him to send me a copy of the contract. I told him that I'd think about it.

He contacted me again several weeks later, when I was playing Doctor Watson to Roger Moore's Sherlock Holmes in *Sherlock Holmes in New York*, at the Fox Studios. I asked him if they were sending a script.

"Oh, don't worry about that," he said. "It's tremendous good news. The series will be every bit as good as *The Avengers*."

I continued to ask them to send a script. They never did, and I went into it with my eyes wide open — despite the comments from an American friend of Diana Rigg, whom I met a few weeks before we started filming. She asked me what I was doing.

"I'm doing this thing called *The New Avengers*," I told her.

"With Diana, of course," she said.

"Well, no," I said hesitantly.

"Then it's not worth doing, is it?!"

Diana grinned. Her friend was not noted for her tact.

Despite this, I really had an instinct to stay with the show — I don't know why, I just did. I've always had a reputation for sticking with things. I stuck with the show for nine years, then did another two years on *The New Avengers* six years later. I was there on the first day and there on the last.

I came back to England with my daughter Jenny. We stayed at The Bull in Gerrards Cross, and then went to see a house in Beaconsfield that I was going to rent for the six months that I was working on the series. The house was lovely and we took it. Jenny stayed around for as long as she could, then flew home.

Being back in England to film *The Avengers* again after six years felt slightly ludicrous. I'd lived a whole life since. I'd played on

The Eagle's Nest

Though we filmed one, a sequence meant to introduce Steed, Purdey and Gambit was dropped from the first *New Avengers* episode. Beautifully crafted by Brain Clemens, here it is, exactly how it appeared in the original script:

TITLE SEQUENCE
The familiar first bars of 'The Avengers Theme' coincide with:

Through the middle of the FROZEN FRAME *bursts* the original logo title of *The Avengers* — coming in with the music and growing larger until it fills screen.

Then: An inverted 'v' and the word 'new' is inserted — both of them scrawled like graffiti — an afterthought. It now reads 'THE new AVENGERS'.

9 CONTINUED:
And with the addenda 'new' — so the music, the NEW music acknowledges the novelty.

AND THROUGH TO:
10 EXT. FIELD. DAY.
LONG SHOT to empty horizon — then, on the horizon, and striding towards us at a good pace is STEED — as we know and remember him best; tall, immaculate, bowler hatted, swinging his umbrella.

CUT TO:
CLOSE SHOT: PANNING WITH STEED as, without slackening his brisk pace, he adjusts his bowler to a jaunty angle and smiles.

SUPERIMPOSE:
"STARRING PATRICK MACNEE as JOHN STEED"

STEED exits shot past CAMERA — and we are HOLDING ON the horizon again — and now, hurrying up into shot come GAMBIT and CHARLY. She is a beat or two behind him, and hurrying to catch up.

CUT TO:
CLOSE SHOT: MIKE GAMBIT — striding along.

SUPERIMPOSE:
"???? as MIKE GAMBIT"

GAMBIT pauses and looks back to where:

CUT TO:
CHARLY has stopped, and bent to lift her skirt to adjust her stocking to its suspender belt. An intimate little moment which will end when she glances up and catches GAMBIT'S eye, and drops her skirt back into place.

SUPERIMPOSE:
"AND ???? as CHARLY"

CHARLY now hurries over to where GAMBIT waits. WE GO WITH HER — she reaches him, and they both look off ahead to where:

CUT TO:
10 CONTINUED:

THEIR EYELINE: STEED — striding away.

CUT TO:
GAMBIT and CHARLY — he glances at her and she, unexpectedly, puts both fingers to her lips and whistles!

CUT TO:
STEED, in DEEP FOREGROUND, stops and turns, then putting his umbrella over his shoulder, he waits while GAMBIT and CHARLY come hurrying over to catch him up.

SUPERIMPOSE:
PRODUCED BY ALBERT FENNELL & BRIAN CLEMENS

They join STEED, exchange smiles — and then, *a team now*, they all turn to stride urgently on. A shot reminiscent of *The Wizard of Oz*.

SUPERIMPOSE:
DIRECTED BY ????

AND THROUGH TO:
11 EXT. HEADLAND. DAY.
FROZEN FRAME OF STANNARD in mid-air. HOLD THIS:

SUPERIMPOSE:
"THE EAGLE'S NEST" BY BRIAN CLEMENS ■

Broadway for two years. I'd been to Australia. I'd been to Canada. I'd toured and done dinner theatre, work that I enjoyed enormously. But there were benefits. I was being given the opportunity to re-explore that wonderful area of Chichester which I'd discovered when playing there in 1975. Working in England is wonderful — there's no better place in the world.

I turned up for the first day at Pinewood studios and was met by Albert Fennell and Brian Clemens, who greeted me with the sort of welcome that I would have loved in the original series. Back then it was, "Come on, get the work done. Go home. See you tomorrow." Now it was, "Hello, Pat. It's *so* good to have you back." I was given a fabulous dressing room, and would I please inform them as to exactly the design and decor I wanted for it?

Then they asked, "Would you come and meet Miss Lumley and Mr Hunt?"

We met in a rehearsal room where Desmond Davis, who was booked to direct the first episode, introduced me to Jo and Gareth.

I was fifty-five at the time and having another great battle with my weight (of which more later), so seeing this beautiful, lustrous young woman sitting there looking at me as though I was God made me feel most peculiar. Jo quite obviously had a wonderful adoration of — *Steed.* I didn't quite know which way to look or what to do.

Gareth did the opposite. He treated me as though I was a fellow rating off a ship. Not in a cocky way, but jauntily, the way that one treats a colleague.

Desmond Davis treated me as though I was James Garner or somebody, which made me feel singularly strange. If the truth be known, I couldn't even remember the original *Avengers* format. I'd spent nine years developing it and six years forgetting it! I felt like a Johnny-Come-Lately.

But what was I thinking of? I'd met these two lovely people and we hit it off from the beginning, which simplified matters. I was determined to give it my best shot.

———

So Steed returned as a semi-retired man with a mansion down near Bracknell. I thought that there was an awful dullness about the scripts, the villains in particular being terribly uninteresting characters. *Trendy* villains in suits with flared trousers, smart shirts and ties, Beatle length hair — all very seventies. Nothing was threatening, exciting or fun, except for Jo and Gareth, two talented and beautiful people.

I cringed when I read the first script and found out that I had a tiny part, a sort of figure in the background as 'Father Steed'. I was longing to say to them, "But you've written

such an awful part for me. I begged you to send me a script. You never did." I said nothing. I smiled and did the work.

We went to Gieves for the clothes. "You need to be dressed, don't you, in the fashion?" they said.

"Oh, I don't think so," I replied, but this chap measured me for a suit and wanted to put flares on my trousers.

"Why do I have to have flares?" I asked him. "Do you remember the old series?"

He shook his head.

"Well, I had *narrow* trousers, with elastic on the bottoms so that they moulded with my Chelsea boots, in a sort of eighteenth century way."

"But it's all flares now, you know. Gareth has flares," he said.

I sighed, looked at him and said, "You know, I don't really care about the *current* fashion. I *set* fashions. I set the fashion I'm requesting now."

So they made me some clothes that looked reasonably good on me, and helped to disguise the fullness of my figure. I hadn't bothered to get the weight off, but I didn't look too bad — or so I thought.

We were then told that we were going to do

Above: Enemy defeated. The New Avengers are off and running — to the tune of Colonel Bogey.

Left: Steed on the fast track.

some location shooting on the Isle of Skye, for the episode 'The Eagle's Nest'. We, the principals, were crossing to Skye by air from Glasgow Airport, the main unit and equipment having gone ahead on the ferry.

Desmond Davis joined us:

'The aircraft was an eight-seater Islander. Pat and Gareth sat in the front seats, behind the pilot, the rest of us took our seats behind them. I watched these heroes of the secret service. They sat pale and silent. They were scared to death and made no secret of it — "Anyone got any Valium?" The pilot revved up the engines, then turned and told us that there was a strong cross wind blowing over the runway at Skye. If it proved too strong on the approach we would have to go back. Everyone nodded in full agreement.

'In his fine Irish accent, the pilot warned us to fasten our seat belts — it would be quite bumpy over the mountains. "Mountains!" said Gareth and looked at Pat.

'Then, as he taxied down the tarmac, "And if any of you's gets nervous, please don't jump out. I don't want to be left all alone up there!" We stared at him in stony silence. We bumped our way across the mountains. I wondered if the heroes were going to be air-sick. No. But they seemed to be regretting the kippers for breakfast.'

We had jolly times there, despite the rain and high winds blowing in off the sea. Peter Cushing joined us and I met Derek Farr, an awfully nice man who suffered (in silence) from arthritis, a result of the war. They were lovely to be with. Peter was always great company. I'd known Peter since 1952, when I worked in a play with him and he'd made me get my hair cut at Olivier's hairdresser, Mr Jones of St James Street. Gareth showed a side to his nature that I'd not seen during that initial introduction, a gift for mimicry (his impersonations of Bogart and Cagney — and Steed — are wicked). And Jo Lumley began to reveal herself as a sweet, incredibly talented, bright and sophisticated lady. We chatted, enjoyed the work and became good mates... *friends*.

As usual when working on location, I spent a great deal of time with the genius behind the show's action sequences, **Ray Austin**:

'Brian had turned us into *The NEW Avengers*. This time we had Purdey — Joanna Lumley — and Gambit — Gareth Hunt. Did I say Diana had long legs? Ha! From time to time Jo took us back to stockings and suspender belts. We would occasionally get a glimpse of stocking tops and cami-knickers as she twirled around in a fight, or kicked out at the bad guys. A sexy

lady. And her action scenes were much tougher than the other girls had to cope with.

'It was the network, I think, who wanted a younger guy to hang around with Purdey. Gareth fitted the bill admirably. A fine actor and, as we soon discovered, a very funny guy (both on and off the set). And drop-dead handsome, as female viewers attest.'

Desmond Davis kept a watchful eye on us throughout the filming:

'I sometimes sat watching the actors between camera set-ups. They usually sat together in a little nest of canvas chairs. Pat was often telling 'actors' stories. I noticed how he was so like Steed off the set, while Gareth and Jo resumed their own distinctive personalities. Pat didn't seem to really act — he just brought Steed on the set with him.

'One day he had a scene where he was buying a fishing rod and reel from a shop. He picked up the rod and expertly demonstrated how the line was thrown. No great heave of the rod, just a flick of the wrist. That was Pat, exactly in character whenever the camera was rolling.'

Maybe so, but at first donning the bowler hat again wasn't as simple as I'd hoped. After the

Left: Locked up by Miller's commandos, Purdey beckons Gambit — with a whistle. From 'Dirtier by the Dozen'.

Opposite above: Purdey and Gambit take to the air in 'Sleeper'.

Opposite below: As we soon discovered, Gareth was a very funny guy both on and off the set.

first couple of days filming, Albert Fennell came to me and said, "Patrick, what's the matter?"

I asked him what he meant.

He said, "Well, you're not Steed."

Whatever did he mean?

He said, "You're not playing the part. You don't seem to be the *character*."

"Oh, aren't I?" I said and asked him to explain. But he couldn't tell me *how* I wasn't playing the part. It all seemed quite unreal.

I offered him the lame excuse that they had taken me by surprise and I should have prepared for it more. It didn't seem to be working and, to make matters worse, I had this fear about over-staying my six months in the country, as I would be double-taxed. And I was overweight, *very* overweight.

Aware of this, Albert knocked the wind out of my sails and conceded that they were trying to find the shots of me that looked, well, *reasonable*!

Oh lummy, I thought. I'd better go away and sort myself out. I knew that I still had *it*, that indefinable ability. I knew that I could still do it, but somewhere along the way I'd forgotten *how* to do it.

A few weeks later, for some unknown reason, (he must have seen one of the original *Avengers* episodes, or read one of the scripts or something), Benny Hill decided to spoof the show in his own inimitable way. He got hold of my tailor, got a bowler hat and umbrella and, in a wickedly funny sketch, gave the most wonderful performance as Steed, every bit as good as my own — nay, *better*. In the background bombs were dropping and everything, but he was on the telephone completely unconcerned about the mayhem that was going on around him. He was suave, insouciant, urbane, sartorial. This dear, sweet man, a truly great comedian who was eventually fired from Thames Television because they said he was too old and sexist, played it absolutely superbly. He played it as *I* had played it. I had found *my* Steed.

———

One weekend, I went to stay with Brian Clemens in his beautiful cottage in Bedfordshire. Brian has always had an ability to make one feel very good about everything. I longed to challenge him about the way they had pared back the role of Steed, but I didn't. We talked about old times, he smoked a cigar or two, Monte Christos I recall, and we shared a bottle of wine. We went on early morning strolls and dined on good food. I enjoyed that most of all, the excitement of visiting friends. Friends like Brian, Ray Austin, who lived with his wife Yasuko in Great Windsor, and Diana Rigg and her husband Archie Stirling, who I visited as often as I could, because they were a

joy to be with.

We held a press launch at The Dorchester Hotel, with Jo, Gareth and myself attending photo call after photo call. Weeks before the series went before the camera, the producers had 'leaked' the word that Purdey would be a stockings and suspenders girl. The press corps picked up on this and wouldn't go away until they'd captured the picture that would grace the front pages of the daily newspapers next morning — the one where Jo is wearing my bowler hat and has a gun tucked into the top of her stocking!

"Show us your suspenders, Joanna," they cried, surging forwards *en masse*. Jo obliged.

Then it was back to the studio and I began to feel like trying to make this thing work. But there is a lot that one has to remember when the cameras are rolling.

As **Desmond Davis** recalls, 'A Day in the Life of John Steed' was full of incident and amusement:

'The camera operator would say: "Pat, would you be a couple of inches more to your left as you come through the door."

'Then, the armourer: "Here's your gun, Pat. Take the safety catch off as you take it out of your pocket. Only blanks."

'Wardrobe (whispering): "Pull your jacket down when you get up or there'll be a nasty crease along the back."

'Director of photography: "Could you lean to your left more as you sit down, Pat, or you will shadow Jo's face."

'Props: "Here's the packet of letters, Pat. I've got ten duplicates in case they don't burn first time."

'Continuity: "Pat, your fork goes down on the plate just as you say 'Really?', just before the grenade lands in your lap!"

'Focus puller: "Pat, I've put a tiny chalk mark for you to hit when you throw yourself on the floor."

'Director: "Come on, lads. Simple shot. Let's go."'

Previously, I couldn't help thinking that we

now had three characters when there really should have been two — after all, three's a crowd — but the show had an awful lot going for it. The photography had an incredible clarity, beautiful colours and wonderful visuals. The dialogue was commendable (despite what I'd originally thought, the jokes didn't interfere with but were incidental to the action). Jo, Gareth and myself had developed a strong rapport. The more we worked as a team, the better we became at it — and though I say it myself, we were quite superb together.

At lunch time I'd sit in the Pinewood studios restaurant and feel a great sense of importance from working there as a star in a major series and still looking good at fifty-five. I felt I had the energy and pride of purpose to make the show work. I felt good.

Little did I know that the programme was about to be sabotaged by the Independent TV network.

The series started showing on ITV, and nobody seemed interested in seeing it. Episodes were shown in various parts of the country at different times for different reasons. I couldn't understand this and I asked a veteran cameraman at Pinewood why it was so. Why weren't we on the way that the old *Avengers* were, at primetime, instead of being seen piecemeal? He didn't know, but suggested that perhaps the show was not as good.

I considered this, as did the critics.

We started well. 'Of all places, the commercial channel should have known how devalued the word 'new' has become: today, it means no more than a slight change of canister round an old, well loved deodorant, a *soupçon* of rabbit essence added to a traditional cats meat recipe,' wrote the writer and critic Alan Coren.

'These *Avengers* are not new at all: the style is exactly what it was a decade ago. Apicella decor, the high-camp detachment of grownups playing children's fantasy games, melodramatic production values achieved by composing shots in glossy James Lobb toecaps and the chromium hubs of the less reliable GT cars, with handheld wobble for taut climaxes and camera teams lying supine the better to shoot up villain's nostrils.

'I like it. I am glad it has not changed at all.'

'Pay no heed to that title. *The New Avengers* are, thank goodness, the old *Avengers*,' reckoned the *Daily Mail* critic Shaun Usher. 'Patrick Macnee, apparently unchanged by time, remains the urbane and unflappable Steed, giving the entertainment a wry flavour with his hint of being a bachelor uncle and man of the world, indulging his young relatives by taking part in sophisticated, melodramatic outdoor charades at a country house weekend.

'Joanna Lumley, as The Girl, is pretty, vivacious, and jolly well-spoken. Gareth Hunt as The Boy, is dark, handsome and terribly dominating, and should play havoc among the impressionable young persons just beginning to outgrow The Bay City Rollers.

'Escapism is the name of *The Avengers'* game, and as pure escapism with outlandish, sub-Hitchcock flourishes, there is nothing quite like it. We've been there before, but the same complaint could be made about most television programmes. At least *The New Avengers* are professional, glossy and knockabout — rather than viciously violent — and the show doesn't take itself seriously.'

Another judged that instead of just being a rehash of the original series, the show camped it up in a different style to even greater effect: 'The absurd and bizarre secret agent plots with suave throwaway lines that out-Bond Bond.

Steed's exaggerated Englishness, Gambit's macho-man posturings, Purdey's leotards and leg action — enormous fun.'

We had our detractors, of course, like the gentleman in the *London Evening News* who compared us to 'a badly-written Brian Rix farce (with apologies to Mr Rix).' Acknowledging that the original series was popular, he maintained that the whole pattern of thriller shows had become far more sophisticated in the intervening years. 'The nonchalant attitude adopted by Patrick Macnee became boring, and whoever thought that Joanna Lumley could act must have a weird sense of humour. Attractive she is, though somewhat shapeless and unfeminine. Actress she is not. All they needed in the cast was Widow Twankey and they would have had a reasonably fourth-rate pantomime!'

Another thought that the new team had lost

Opposite above: Super man, super machine.

the magical on-screen chemistry which was central to *The Avengers* and never quite managed to recreate the weirdness and essentially English eccentricity of the original.

So while the critics were giving us a chance, the programme schedulers had squandered our shot at success.

No longer being on the network filled me with a feeling of great emptiness. Pouring oil on troubled waters, I started drinking again. I've always had that typically awful British inability — personified by people like me — of being unable to say, "Things aren't quite right, are they?" and instead just let it go on in the hope that it would get better.

Throughout this time I'd managed to maintain a cottage in Runcton, near to Chichester, where I kept all the things I'd gathered the year before when I appeared in the play by Andrew Sachs. So it was a great relief to get away from it all at weekends, when I'd drive to West Wittering and walk along the beach.

Towards the end of the first period of filming, I went with my friend Marie Cameron to the Windsor Rep to see a play. During the interval, I told the theatre company that I'd done *Sleuth* on Broadway for two years. They were thinking of putting it on again. Would I play it? Because I was uncertain as to whether I would be in the country that long, I said, "I can't come and play it for you now, but... eventually, yes. I'd love to."

I never did, of course. Patrick Cargill did it instead, was an enormous success and went on to play at the Strand Theatre for quite a long time... for such a long time, in fact, that, finally, they asked me to play it in 1978. Would I take over from him at the end of *his* run! So, whereas I could have been in the West End doing this, that and the other, I always baulked. I didn't do this, I didn't do that. My business manager was always telling me, "Patrick, you shouldn't take this one, because..." or, "No, Patrick, this one is wrong for you, because..."

Anyway, after completing thirteen episodes of *The New Avengers*, I returned to Palm Springs.

I lived with my daughter Jenny for the remainder of 1976. She got me on the salads, ushered me out of the door for early morning walks and I took off forty pounds. Then I whizzed off to Swaziland and acted in a strange film called *King Solomon's Treasure*, for producer Harry Alan Towers. It was (loosely) based on the H. Rider Haggard novel *King Solomon's Mines*, and I rode a horse and spent a great deal of time on it in an admiral's uniform. I appeared with David McCallum, Britt Ekland and John Colicos, from Canada. I remember that we used to go from one location

to the other on horseback. I hadn't ridden for years. It was a lovely break.

Then I flew back to Palm Springs. I was just lazing about and quite enjoying life, when plans were made for me to take over from Anthony Perkins in a tour of *Equus*, the play by Peter Shaffer. This was arranged because we didn't expect *The New Avengers* to be picked up.

However, my agent John Redway phoned and told me that they were going to start filming again. This time, I made my voice heard and laid down a few conditions. I spoke to Brian Clemens and said, "Unless you can make this character better, what the hell's the point in having me in the series? Why don't you do it with just the two of them, Joanna and Gareth?"

I went to stay with him again. We spent some time together and Brian gradually got a hold on the part as I wanted to play it. He added a strength and purpose to Steed so that in the second thirteen episodes I figure more strongly than I did in the first thirteen, which was pleasing to me — as was the fact that I was much slimmer and extraordinarily fit.

So it was back to Pinewood and more weekend visits to Diana Rigg and Archie Stirling. Diana was just about to have her baby. I spent a lot of time with them, dining and chatting.

Every minute in their company was a sheer joy, while days at the studio had their highs and lows.

————

The second series of *The New Avengers* seemed to be progressing quite well and we made some very good episodes. One of the best, I think, was 'Dead Men Are Dangerous', written by Brian Clemens, which added colourful brush strokes to Steed's canvas.

Jo had become a celebrity by this time, of course, largely because of the hairstyle she had invented, which she called 'The Purdey Bob'. She looked stunning. Gareth had conquered women's hearts. They were enjoying every minute of it, but I felt depressed.

Somehow though, one's resilience and stamina were still there and I was always able, through some sort of extraordinary ego, to force my way, eventually, to the top. Then, whenever I got to the top, I found a way of getting hold of a rope and just hanging myself. It was the total opposite of the way one is supposed to feel when at the top of one's profession. When *I* reached the top, I looked down and got vertigo. That's why, oddly enough, *The New Avengers* was, from my point of view, ineffective, because *I'd* lost all that wonderful energy.

Above: Joanna, Gareth and myself pictured with 'Purdey' look-alikes, at a TV Times award ceremony.

Opposite above: Relaxing on set with a shoot-'em-up novel.

Above: On location in Paris.

Right: Working on location leaves you open to the elements, hence the jacket.

I talked to Ray Austin about this. He just told me to get on with it: "You worry too much." Perhaps I did, but I couldn't stop thinking that everything seemed to be in too much of a hurry. We were always shooting two or three shows back to back, and sometimes we actually shot four! I thought there wasn't enough exploration in the plots. I felt that even then, which is twenty years ago now, we could have used ESP or inter-communication between each other with computer technology. We didn't. We'd done much more than that in the original *Avengers*, but in *The New Avengers*, instead of being fractionally ahead of our time, we were behind it. I pushed for the ESP angle in *The New Avengers*, because people who are very close to each other do have a tremendous psychic communication. So these so-called undercover people, spies or whatever we were, *could* have found a way to use this strange extra-sensory perception to their advantage. We almost got it in 'Cat Amongst the Pigeons', the episode about a man who has the power to make birds do his bidding.

After several months filming, we were told

that we would be shooting a few episodes in France.

"Oh, that's rather exciting," we said. It wasn't. The time there was a social strain. Jo, Gareth and myself stayed at the Hilton Hotel in Paris, and every weekend I would go down to Cannes on my own, at Rudolph Roffi's expense. I remember him taking me to Tour D'Argent, a famous and unashamedly capitalist restaurant in Paris, and telling me that he was a communist!

We filmed three shows in France, none of which were all that good. The cameraman we had was the chap who had done *Emmanuelle*, the soft-porn film. He kept insisting on putting four black silk stockings over the lens. Finally we got him down to just two!

During this time the weight crept back on and during the final days of filming in Paris I'd started to drink again. A glass of white wine became wine with this, wine with that, wine for wine's sake and, before I knew it, it was a bottle with the lunch. I didn't know that I was doing myself any damage — I certainly didn't know about sugar and fat and cholesterol. I didn't *care* really, I just lived for the moment. So my pain was self-indulgent.

Gareth Hunt recalls that Gambit had pain thrust upon him from an entirely different source:

'So here I was in Paris having acquired the part of Gambit in *The New Avengers* after being chosen from a large number of actors. I was feeling great. It had been arranged that the press were to take publicity pictures of me being disarmed by a professor of French kick-boxing. He wore a red leotard and black swimming trunks and carried a cane. The 'script' called for me to point a Smith and Wesson .45 at the press. "Hold the gun," said the professor. So I did. Swish! His cane came down on my wrist. The gun went flying. Thwack, he clipped me round the left ear. It hurt.

'Then we did it again, for the photographers.

'This time he hit me behind my right ear. Then to prove a point, he kicked the gun out of my hand and booted me in the family jewels! The cameras flashed. The photographers cheered. Pat and Jo, watching from the sidelines, exploded with laughter. They might well have seen the funny side of things — sore-groin Hunt most certainly didn't!'

At this time things started to go wrong in the financial quarter. The show's finances had apparently been going awry for quite some time, but we didn't really know about this. We were employed, and kept telling ourselves that things would be all right. Tomorrow is another day.

Above: On location in Ontario, Canada.

Opposite below: Cybernaut Felix Kane (Robert Lang) proves to be a pain in the neck.

The first whiff we had that things weren't right was when Jo popped into Albert Fennell's office to ask a favour. She wanted some time off, just a couple of hours, to visit a show called *Very Good Eddie* with a friend. That's when we found out that they weren't going to pay us — they being the foreign backers.

Apparently the problem lay with capricious international banking arrangements. Indeed, I remember Brian Clemens explaining to the press how the money to pay our wages had actually been moved around the world, from places as far apart as Guatemala and Switzerland!

They didn't pay us until three months later, when our agents cried, "Foul!" The onus of paying us fell upon Albert Fennell and Brian Clemens, who dipped deep into their own pockets and paid the three of us a weekly stipend, an extremely generous gesture. They, too, were owed money. From that time forwards, *Very Good Eddie* was affectionately referred to as *Very* Bad *Eddie*.

Finally, we went to Canada in a last ditch attempt to keep the show alive. We checked in at the Harbour Castle Hotel, in Toronto — and had a perfectly awful time of things.

The money for these episodes was put up by the *Toronto Star* newspaper, and we had just enough capital to finish off the second batch of thirteen shows and complete the complement of twenty-six episodes. Then the money ran out and we finally finished the series while on location in Toronto's South Humber Park. It was a great shame because I was then spending a lot of time with my son, Rupert, who lived in the city.

Like me, Jo Lumley was someone who had been brought up in the English public school system. Consequently she was used to public school punishment and discipline and had learned to put up with it — until, one day, she didn't!

Ingrained deep in my memory are three instances when Purdey's *purr* became a growl, and Gambit's technique brought the house down — well, almost.

One took place in Paris, during a huge dinner party. Everyone who meant anything was gathered around the table: the French backer, the French producer, Ray Austin, who was representing the interests of the British producers, Jo, myself and Gareth. Jo, in front of the whole table, climbed to her feet and said, "The only trouble with this series, is that *we* work while others play!" There was a terrible hush.

She was right. *I* should have been the one to say it, of course. I didn't. I didn't even have the guts to express my agreement and shout, "Hear! Hear!" As ever, Macnee was a coward.

Gareth Hunt tells his own story:

'I spent the first day in Toronto going through windows. We were filming in a mansion in Rosedale, which the owner had kindly lent us for the day. (He wasn't very pleased at the end of it.) The director decided that in order to see me through the glass, I needed to stand quite close to it. I tried to explain to him that in order to get through the glass I would have to be travelling at quite a speed, do a forward roll and come up with the gun pointing.

'He'd also decided that the effect would be better if the curtains remained drawn — well, at least slightly apart. I explained that on coming through the window there was a strong possibility that I would pull them down. After much prodding and pulling, verbals in French and English, I went through on the shorter run, split my head open and yanked down the rather expensive curtains.

'It was a fake window, of course, sugar glass. But I still cut myself. Unfortunately, the room was decked out with a fluffy white carpet onto which I, alas, was now spilling my blood! The house owner was not a very happy bunny at all.

'I remember Patrick saying, "Dear boy, the

biggest stunt *I* ever do is getting in and out of the car."'

The final instance of Jo's growl occurred just outside Toronto. We knew the worst then, and I have a lasting impression of Jo, dressed in a miniskirt, walking across a large field. She paused for a moment to pick up a daisy or something, picked up her pace and went thundering off out of camera range, followed by Ray Austin, bent double, trying to keep up with her.

"Joanna," he called. "Joanna!"

She stopped, briefly, turned to look at him and said, "I'm never coming back!" And then she disappeared.

She did return, of course. A trouper like Jo would do nothing less. She came back, completed her scenes, and that was the end of it, *The New Avengers* was put away.

It's only lately, through listening to Joanna Lumley's autobiography on tape, that I found out an awful lot I hadn't known before about why the show finally expired, by reason of lack of funds, a few weeks later in, of all

places, Toronto.

If one accepts the premise I made earlier — that *The Avengers* was the brainchild of Toronto-born Sydney Newman — it is perhaps fitting that the show ended its days in the home of its creator.

———

I didn't see Jo and Gareth again until Sunday 23 September 1984, although we kept in touch. Eamonn Andrews brought us together again, outside a London hotel. I was there, I thought, to have some publicity pictures taken, before flying back to California. In the company of Jo and Gareth, Eamonn escorted me to the waiting limousine — a vintage green Bentley, hired for the occasion — and we drove off for the Royalty Theatre, in Portugal Street, where *This is Your Life* — my own, this time — was to be filmed.

My feet had hardly touched the ground when Eamonn said, "Well, Patrick, I know I couldn't have been in better company when I surprised you just now because, like so many people you've worked with in your long career, Joanna and Gareth became not just colleagues but good friends... as did three stunning star assistants going back twenty-three years, who are not here on stage with you tonight, only because professional demands prevented them, and they crash-bang-walloped onto our screens like this..."

Clips of Honor, Diana, Linda, Joanna and myself filled the television monitor screen and a tear formed in the corner of my eye.

"And Patrick," said Eamonn, breaking my reverie, "even if those various stars are working in places as far apart as New York, London and Scotland tonight, they still greet you on screen... and warmly, as you can see from the very first — Cathy Gale." In rapid succession, Honor, Diana and Linda appeared to send me greetings (I wasn't to know that Honor was actually in the studio all the time, waiting to make her entrance in true Cathy Gale style — on a 750cc motorcycle!)

The biggest surprise was kept until the end — my mum! Ninety-five years young, she passed away ten weeks later. God bless her. ∎

Above: From left to right: my brother Jimmy, first wife Barbara, Honor, Leslie Philips, my mum (kept until the end as a delightful surprise!), my son Rupert, Patrick Cargill, Gareth, David Greene and Ian.

Opposite above: In the company of Jo and Gareth, Eamonn Andrews produces the Big Red Book.

People ask me, did playing Steed harm my career? Well, I'm not a great actor. I could have achieved a great deal more than I ever did, but all too often I would run away from the real challenge. I was happier on the slopes than on the heights.

I remember when Tony Quayle wrote me a letter after I'd turned down *Sleuth* in London in 1970. When in 1972 I was offered it again on Broadway, Tony insisted, "This part is made for you. *Do it!* If you miss your opportunity now you'll never forgive yourself." And he was right. But my own nature told me that I couldn't do it. A few of the critics told me that I didn't perform it as well as Quayle, Paul Rogers or other people who came before me, but I finally made it the longest running thriller on Broadway! I then took it on tour up and down the East coast of the United States and won the Straw Hat Award. (A most peculiar sort of trophy, my mother kept it for many years in the public bar at the Methuen Arms in Corsham and, in fact, had many drinks and lived off the memory of the award.)

Nevertheless, one always had the feeling that... well, as Peter O'Toole said to me, "But, Patrick, you're *always* doing *The Avengers*!" And I was. That was my finest hour, my *Valiant Years* if you like, but I never really appreciated it at the time. I considered those years as part of my progress towards becoming a *successful* actor. The success that I had was actually *then*, but I didn't realise it.

I should have known that *The Avengers* was not going to last forever. If I'd started to plan ahead — as Roger Moore advised me to do, to have ideas for a project to follow on immediately — I wouldn't have lost my place in the hierarchy of English actors. But then I wouldn't have gravitated to Palm Springs, where I've been living since 1969 and which has been so good for me!

I certainly don't consider my career to have been limited, although my one major success was *The Avengers*. So, no, *The Avengers* didn't type me negatively. It *made* my career and allowed me to do lots of other things. I take great pride in recalling that I could open in a play on Broadway, or in London's West End, and fill a theatre on the strength of my name — *Steed's* name.

The Avengers, or *Chapeau Melon et Bottes de Cuir* (as the show is known in France), or *Mit Schirm*

Charme und Melone* (in Germany), or *Los Vengerdores* (in Spain), allowed me to become known internationally. When I meet people, they don't have to ask if I'm a doctor or an engineer. "Hello Steed!" they say. It's a wonderful thing. It gives me a sort of fellowship throughout the world — that's the joy of being an actor.

———

I've been watching Orson Welles talking on *Parkinson* about actors.

"Actors really aren't anything, are they?" said Welles.

Well of course he's wrong, because he wasn't really a very good *actor* anyway, although he probably directed the greatest film ever made. What he did have was an extraordinary mind

Above: With Roger Moore, on the set of the film The Sea Wolves.

Opposite: Sleuth. *A few of the critics told me that I didn't play it as well as Quayle or Rogers, or people before me. But I finally made* Sleuth *the longest running thriller on Broadway.*

LIFE AFTER THE AVENGERS

*I've always said that
none of the women
I worked with
attracted me...*

and remarkable perception. He unearthed techniques, visions and ideas with his wonderful galvanic brain. His stage production of *Othello*, on the other hand, which I saw from the third row of the stalls at the St James Theatre around 1950, was one great rumbling bore! Peter Finch was in it. He hopped about as Iago... it was all bad.

I was with Welles in a film called *Three Cases of Murder* in 1953, and he was directing his segment while poor old George More O'Ferrall (who'd been hired to direct) had to sit on the sidelines in his director's chair and do nothing.

Welles was a gargantuan show-off of the best kind, with an extraordinary, resonant voice. His scorn for actors was really to put them in their place, because the actors he had scorn for were better than him.

Now, to me, to be an *actor* is not to know your limitations. That's why I have such inestimable regard for Paul Scofield, for Donald Sinden, for Robert Stephens — God rest his soul — for Ian McKellen, and particularly for Michael Gambon and Brian Bedford.

People don't realise that actors are always looked upon and talked about in a rather disparaging way, by writers, lawyers, doctors — any number of people who have *just* managed to acquire sufficient skill to do what they do, while the best actors make it look inspirational. Good actors, *great* actors, make it look as though it came from nowhere.

The technique is to become seamed into the performance. It's like a beautiful piece of Chippendale furniture. You don't draw attention to yourself. You have to instil into yourself an incredible discipline — to endure the pain, the digging, the flailing about. Flailing, trying, standing in front of the mirror looking idiotic, doing whatever you can to wrench

something out of whatever the script says.

As Olivier used to say, to be an actor you need "extraordinary stamina!" Every limb, the stomach, the shoulders, the neck muscles, the flexibility of your knees and ankles, need to be exemplary and immediate. To be an actor takes, first of all, ego — ego in the correct sense. You have to feel that it's only *you* doing it. You don't think about anybody else.

Let me look at acting in terms of what I did in *The Avengers*. The reason I succeeded was because it never occurred to me for a moment that what I was doing was wrong, or what I was doing was right. To me, you see, the happiest form of exposition is what I call acting 'in parentheses'. My best work in *The Avengers* was done 'in parentheses', flying off at a wild tangent.

I would say some unutterably boring lines about what we were doing, or attempting to do, and then suddenly say, "I had an Aunty like that." You'd throw things away in the Beatrice Lillie sense; hurl it away so everybody notices that more than what you were really saying at the start. (It has developed, in my old age, into eccentricity. I can go on talk shows and when somebody asks me some damned silly question, I suddenly go off and extol the virtues of hanging on to one's prostate!)

This isn't necessarily *the* right way to act. What's important is believing you're right, otherwise you can't act at all. If you go around asking people, "What do you think? How do you think I should do it?" — you're sunk.

I remember that people used to undercut me when I was at Windsor Rep. They'd say, "Well, you're handsome and all that, but you're not very *good*, are you?" They were better actors, of course — there are always 'better' actors, like Patrick Cargill and Leslie Philips — and

they walked in and took away my position because I gave it up voluntarily, as I didn't think that I was good enough and I'd better get more practice somewhere else.

So I am not a good actor.

And yet at moments I'm a supreme actor. I had *two minutes*, at one matinee in *Sleuth* on Broadway, in which I was sublime. Occasionally in *The Avengers* I carried it through. There's the one about the clowns, 'Look — (stop me if you've heard this one) But There Were These Two Fellers...' in which I do some chat to Linda Thorson, while driving along lauding the merits of flowers metamorphosing into bananas, which I did in a quite extraordinary way.

I remember in Australia, in *The Secretary Bird*, being absolutely, exquisitely good. I imagine at certain times with Diana Rigg I was good — and yet all the time I felt inferior, because I was brought up to feel inferior. But then that's quite good for an actor, because you strive even harder.

The part or the role is supreme — and suddenly *The Avengers* offered me the part supreme, and I went for it. But I didn't consciously feel that I was going for it. Because I'd been acting for so long, I didn't need to think about it. I just went in there and *did* it as I always had: Peter Hammond tried to tell me *how* to do it — to be polite, accurate and correct — and then had to finally throw up his hands and say, "No. Do it *your* way."

To be an actor is a thing of enormous pride. I love other actors.

When I say how wonderfully Paul Scofield acts, only a few of us notice how well he does it. Such great actors are able to conjure up emotions. The point is, if you say that Olivier was great (because he was great!), you can't then say

I can't be great, *I* can't reach those heights.

I *could*, in a light-comedy way. I couldn't do it nearly as well as Rex Harrison, but in *Sleuth* I went up and down those stairs and did it just like Rex Harrison. I have a feeling that if I had taken over from Anthony Quayle at the St Martin's Theatre, in London in 1970, they might well have considered me for the film.

I have an ability, a sort of naturalism, to take dialogue and weave one sentence into another. Andre Morrell was terrific at it in *Arms and the Man*, at going through a speech and linking one stanza into another. The way we talk, the way we *don't* put in the full stops is barely a conscious thought. It just goes through one's head and comes out. But then there are the technical aspects of acting. Olivier used to direct, "Four paces forward. Four to the right..." Why? Because there have to be 'rules of the road', which must be acknowledged. But on the other hand, the *rush* of the emotion, the moment of exultation, is tremendously satisfying.

And when we apply it, on the stage, in film or on television — not always in the starring role — we take over the audience. In the successes I've had, I've done that. The occasions where suddenly one was deaf for six weeks, through an infection, or one wasn't up to it, or one had rows with the director — they were the important times, when you had to bring in what they call magnetism, the process of *willing* the whole audience, from just over the footlights to the back of the house, to be with *you*. Any actor who has controlled an audience from the stage knows that you can do it in film too. He knows that feeling of control, of willing and holding the people out there like a magnet and saying, *"Look at me. Listen to me. Feel with me"* — of appealing to a group

Right: Reunited at the launch of The Avengers *on video, October 1993.*

Above: With Oasis, during the filming of the video for their song 'Don't Look Back in Anger'. My contribution was minimal and tinged by my sense of humour. I agreed to send myself up by driving a London taxi, and peered furtively around corners, twirling an umbrella in a Steed-esque manner.

through one's own magnetism.

What really matters — the *only* thing that conceivably matters in acting — is what you do in front of the camera. That's golden, but only *you* know it.

I know nothing technical. When someone says, "Rolling," I presume that's when the film is going through the camera. When someone says, "Action," you're *on*. Acting is not, as some people think, showing off. You're not showing off — you're illuminating. You're illuminating an area, putting a light on things where there wasn't light before. And when you share it with someone like Honor, Diana, Linda or Joanna, it's an absolutely golden time. Your memory digs down into your emotions, wherever those happen to be. They're not in the body. They're in parts of your soul. There's a sort of religious aspect to it, an unexplainable *knowledge*.

People say, "How do you learn all those lines?" Well, that's really like asking, "How do you walk without putting shoes on?" The basics are so ordinary. It's the subtleties that are so wonderful. To look in the eyes and say one thing when you mean another. Hiding, changing, inflecting.

That's what's so marvellous about acting, and an actor is a totally different animal from what the average person thinks.

When you see an actor and an actress getting it *right* together, it's a wonderful thing — and I did that with four of the most beautiful, talented actresses in the business. Honor, Diana, Linda and Joanna — *they* were the attraction. *They* made *The Avengers*.

I love them all, dearly.

————

I've always said that none of the women I worked with attracted me in a physical sense. That, of course, was my way of describing something that I felt deeply about but haven't, until now, cared to admit.

Honor Blackman I was hugely attracted to. As misinterpreted in my book *Blind in One Ear*, when she came to my mews flat just before we began production of the taped episodes, we had a *slightly* sensual moment. Then she quickly pointed out that she was married and that was the end of it. "Thanks very much. I'm looking forward to working with you," and she was gone.

Diana Rigg turned me on so madly that I had to channel my thoughts to other things. I adored her when she wore those catsuits and flicked back her gorgeous auburn hair. Her flashing eyes and the total physicality of being near her drove me to distraction... but I never, ever made an approach. She was completely her own woman — and told me many times that she really had to be with a man of intellect!

At times... well, quite a lot actually, Linda Thorson turned my head and set my libido racing. A wonderful wild card, she had the natural exuberance and vigour of youth... but I was too old. I never felt less than heated with Joanna Lumley, but she was far too occupied with someone else... and again, I was far too old. On an intellectual level, of course, they made me want to talk to them, relate to them and be with them.

So *all* the women quite definitely turned me on, but enormous self-control and the discipline instilled into one at public school as to what one should do — or shouldn't do — with a woman stopped me from doing anything.

It's perfectly obvious from the things we did together in *The Avengers* that a great deal of the androgynous sexuality delighted me. I loved every minute of it. It was *fun*!

————

It's now over thirty-five years since I made that first episode with Ian Hendry, but *The Avengers*, and Steed, live on. The programme is still being shown around the world and has been immensely popular on home video. And, of course, there's been talk of a Hollywood film version for years now. It's true to say, I think, that the show has become a part of our culture. It had a look and a style which is still unique — and much imitated. A good example is the video that The Pretenders made for their single 'Don't Get Me Wrong'. Cast as an Emma Peel/Tara King lookalike, and dressed in a colourful array of pop-art outfits worthy of an *Avengers* heroine, singer Chrissie Hynde — a great admirer of *The Avengers* — paid us a glowing tribute. Wonderful in its dedication to detail, one could be forgiven for believing that when Steed peers through his apartment window as the new *Avengers* girl parks her car next to the Bentley in 'Stable Mews' and ascends the staircase for a 'face to face' rendezvous, it was for real. It wasn't though, as we weren't even on the same continent at the time — the effect being achieved by discerning use of excerpts from the episode 'The Forget-Me-Knot'.

On 26 October 1993, twenty-three years after we had ceased production of the original *Avengers* series, I was reunited with all three of my leading ladies for the first time. The venue, a secret location in London. The occasion, the release of *The Avengers* on video.

Attending were Honor Blackman, Linda Thorson and Diana Rigg, who graciously gave up several hours of her leisure time before having to race away for the curtain call of her award-winning performance in *Medea*.

Being together for the first — and possibly only — time was wistful and nostalgic.

I'm sometimes asked what the biggest influence has been in my life. When I was younger I didn't think that anyone had any particular influence, because they were all so contradictory and cancelled each other out.

Then, suddenly, fifteen years ago, in Palm Springs all that changed. A *real* influence came into my life — my darling, Hungarian wife Baba, the first woman I have ever *allowed* myself to love. And who loves me.

Also, I'm still working, at seventy-four years of age! I have been presenting a series called *Mysteries, Magic and Miracles* on the Sci-Fi and Discovery Channels for the last two years, and start a new one, *Ghost Stories*, on the NBC network this year.

A new TV series, *Spy Game* on the ABC network, opens soon in which I play a retired rogue spy. It is fun to be working with very talented, *young* people, and the leading spy does *not* carry a gun! In the present vio-

lent world of television, I find that very refreshing.

The stage is another matter! Arthritis, the physical manifestation of years of mild to moderate excess, has entered the scene. Rex Harrison is supposed to have turned down the leading part in *Sleuth* because he didn't want to run up and down "any more of those stairs." I spent two years playing the part on Broadway, running up and down those stairs over and over again, eight times a week. As a result, I can still run *upstairs*, but my knees won't allow me to come down again!

So, alas, the stage — many stages in all parts of the world — is now only a rich and fulfilling memory.

Nevertheless, I *love* life and it has been kind to me.

Life is good. ∎

Left: With my son Rupert and daughter Jenny, June 1995.

Above: With my darling wife, Baba.